5-

Maria, april 2014
May this book
inspire you on your
journey with J.C!
Love you
+ Shannon

LET IT BE

LET IT BE

Katie Scott

Dedication

For my daughters, Susan and Sophia, your genuine love and innocent observations enlighten me and fuel me to push forward. I pray that my actions teach you to always trust in God. To my loving parents, Susan and David Ridgeway, your example taught me that although life may bring hardships, true love will carry you through the storms. To my brothers, Patrick, Michael and Christopher, thank you for always watching over me. I love you! To my amazing husband, partner and best friend, Stanton Scott, thank you for waiting forty years for me! It is complete joy to share life, happiness and an abundance of love with you and our precious family. Your love is a gift and it continues to shine forth through our children, Stella and Shepherd. Jesus, I trust in You!

Introduction

I am an interior designer by trade, and it wasn't until I experienced a spiritual urging, encouraging me to write that my direction in life would drastically change. The suggestion was confusing to me in the sense that I have never had the desire to write, nor am I gifted in this area. It was unexpected in that my interior design career was just beginning to take off. I thought, "Why would God be directing me to write?" Regardless of my personal doubts, the encouragement to *write* consistently pressed strongly on my heart, and I finally surrendered to the still, small voice that spoke inside of me. Perplexed as to what the subject matter should be, I began penning the details of my spiritual quest. Unknowingly, I *was* working on an "interior" design job: I was documenting the renovation of my soul, and the gift of peace and love that I found through learning to trust in God. The glory of a renovation is turning something broken into something beautiful. This is the story of my design from within, a classic and timeless renovation.

February 11, 2008

I had been crying most of the day. My marriage of nearly ten years was broken. Contention did not appear overnight, and the challenges we faced had been present for years. We attended marriage counseling over a period of time. It is not as if I was giving up on a whim, yet the reality of my circumstances continuing to take a downward spiral could not be ignored. The thought of being a divorced young woman with two daughters, Susan, age seven and Sophia, age four, was enough to make my stomach flip ferociously, weaken every limb in my body and make me feel physically ill. Although I was afraid, I knew it was time to break the cycle that would not end. I was trying desperately to pull myself together as I drove to a scheduled meeting. Making tile selections for an entire house was furthest from my heart. Regardless, I knew I had to push forward, dry my tears and ignore the red, swollen eyes that stared back at me in the rearview mirror.

I had reached my destination and as I was rallying myself together, my phone rang. I glanced down and did not recognize the area code. I had no time, nor the energy to talk to a stranger, until something inside of me urged, "Answer the phone." I hesitated, reached out and spoke in a nasal tone, "Hello." "Hi, my name is Kristen, and I am with *domino* magazine. Is this Katie Stassi?" I was curious, and I answered quickly, "Yes, this is Katie." "Congratulations," she said, "You have been selected as a '*domino* 10'. This is our second annual contest, and we select, whom we believe to be the next up and coming top ten designers in the nation. If you accept, we would like to feature you and nine others in the April, 2008 issue of *domino* magazine." Kristen continued, "We need to work quickly as we do not have much time. If you accept, can we schedule a phone interview with you tomorrow?"

The news hit me like a strong ray of sunshine, and I responded, "Absolutely! What time?"

The interview was set, and I thought I was ready until they asked me the very first question: "Where did you receive your training?" My heart sank, and I thought I would immediately be disqualified when they found out about my *lack* of credentials. I did not have a formal degree in interior design, I have never worked or studied under another designer, and I am not ASID certified. Regardless, I knew I had to tell the truth, and I slowly spoke "It is a gift from God." The only sound that resonated between the phone lines was silence. I sat in anticipation of being disqualified until I finally heard her respond, "That is beautiful. I love it!"

The April, 2008 issue recognized me as a "*domino* 10" and gave credit to my talent as "A gift from God." My dream of being a published interior designer finally came true. Immediately, my phone began to ring and readers from all over the world flooded my inbox. To my surprise, it was not just my interior design style that readers admired, it was my response to the question regarding my training that attracted so many callers. Readers found it refreshing I gave credit to God. They wanted to know how I discovered my natural talent, and whether I could help them discover their own. I soon realized I was more inspired to inspire others to discover and utilize their God-given gifts. In an instant, my heart went from interior design to in+terior design. I wanted to help others, but I knew that first I would have to learn how to help myself.

To date, I had used my gift of design to style and create my house and environment in a way that reflected how *I wanted to feel on the inside*. I had the talent to create my surroundings to stage my emotions. My house was simple, clean, fresh and grounded in tradition, yet it revealed unexpected touches to reflect the beauty found in balancing diversity, which leads to creativity, excitement and an element of surprise. I longed to feel love and live in a paradise of peace, tranquility and adventure. My design would serve as an escape from reality and the commotion that life delivers.

The design of my house was complete, and it was everything I had ever wished for. I loved my house! The problem was the feelings my house and environment were supposed to create were only temporary and fleeting. I wanted these feelings to last a lifetime. I recognized that it was my in+terior that was not complete, and that my interior design skills could never fulfill or serve that purpose.

It is my belief that God reveals Himself to each of us in the way in which we perceive Him. While I may be a professional at renovating and restoring homes, God soon showed me He is the professional at renovating and restoring souls.

Reflection

I made the decision that a marital separation was inevitable. On May 31, 2008, my two daughters and I relocated from Houston, Texas to my hometown of New Orleans, Louisiana. I had been commuting between Houston and New Orleans to assist in caring for my dad. On February 16, 2008, my father nearly passed away due to a massive cerebral hemorrhage, and he was left critically ill and physically handicapped. I thought it would be beneficial for me and my daughters to live with my parents for the summer; I would help my mother care for my dad, and in return, my family would be a good support for us during a difficult time.

Although my husband was not happy with my decision to separate and live in New Orleans, he allowed me to relocate for the summer with our two daughters. He stayed in Houston where he was employed.

Almost immediately after our separation, our broken relationship further deteriorated. We were at complete odds. We continued to argue over the same issues that challenged us for years. From my perspective, we were past the point of no return, and it was time to end our marriage. I also recognized that despite all of the turmoil and commotion erupting in *all* areas of my life, I was finally at peace.

By the end of July 2008, divorce proceedings were in motion. I was told that if we could both agree to all of the terms, according to Texas law, we could be divorced in sixty days. I wanted all of us, including Matt, my soon to be ex-husband, to live in New Orleans. My thinking was shortsighted, and our occupation's and finances were at the very bottom of my priority list. I knew that by leaving Houston, the security in our job's would be gone, and my focus was on only one point: it's better for us to live in a city where both of our families reside. I thought New Orleans would provide a stronger sense of family, being that we would be surrounded by family, although our unit was being torn apart.

My big interior design jobs dwindled with the global economic meltdown. I was a single mom barely able to make ends meet, my soon to be ex-husband moved to New Orleans to be closer to his children, and my father was literally helpless. My parents could not assist me financially, but they provided shelter for us. We lived with them while I tried to re-establish myself. I took any little interior design job that came my way. My *domino* 10 status was not beneficial to me at this point because when people need to cut expenses, interior designers are on the top of the list. Designers are a luxury in life, not a necessity in life. I had worked so hard to get to that point in my career, and now I was starting all over again.

Although my marriage had failed, I was not ready to give up on love. I was determined to give and receive love with a healthy heart and experience inner peace every day. I wanted to learn to walk through life gracefully, even in the midst of a storm. My big question to God was "How do I do this?"

12/05/08

"I HAVE SOMETHING BEAUTIFUL PLANNED FOR YOU."

Last night a message was delivered to me. It was spoken in a slow, loving and calm gentleman's voice, "Patience. I need for you to be patient. Patient." I woke from my sleep feeling like I was in a mesmerized and hypnotic state as I murmured the word, "patient." I had the wisdom and insight to recognize it was the Spirit of Jesus speaking to me. I confirmed His message to me by acknowledging His advice. He told my heart, "I have something beautiful planned for you." I was to trust Him, and wait patiently for His plan to come together. I fell peacefully back to sleep.

I woke again as I heard myself speaking out loud to Jesus, "It is all about peace. Peace is everything." I told Him that peace was all that mattered to me—feeling and experiencing His peace. With peace comes love. With peace comes simplicity. With peace comes ease. With peace comes gratitude. With peace comes clarity. With peace comes acceptance. I fell back asleep again.

Waking for the third and final time, I was enthusiastically collaborating with Jesus, I said, "What about faith, hope and trust?" I remember feeling very excited. My alarm went off at 5:00 a.m. I was so thrilled to get out of bed, and I felt an unusually strong bond with Jesus. I *knew* His Spirit was present, and He had been coaching me throughout the night. What a gift!

This dream I am referring to was unlike any other dream. I couldn't see any visuals. I could only hear softly spoken words that were very direct. I felt like I was training for an assignment; it was the triathlon of life. It is a course that will change, a course that can be unpredictable, and a course for which I was to prepare for. The training requires daily discipline and exercising trust in God at all times.

When I pray and meditate on Jesus, I reach my surrender to God. I know this because I can sense His presence—the air around me suddenly begins to feel very full, warm and loving. I began to notice that this "sense" appears in unison with certain thoughts that I present to Jesus, or that He presents to me. I interpret it as the Holy Spirit's way of encouraging my soul to pay attention to that particular thought and/or feeling. An example of this experience is the time I heard a small voice from within simply say, "Write." Simultaneously, I felt a presence lingering around me in a sweet and caring way. I recognize this feeling to be Jesus's way of letting me know that He is *really* with me, and He is *speaking* to my heart. The feeling is overwhelmingly beautiful, peaceful and loving. I realized there is nothing to be frightened by. It is simply feeling genuinely loved, feeling full, feeling inner peace and having an awareness that what I am being instructed to do is authentic. This is His way of giving me the confidence I need to follow His direction.

At random times during the day, I will focus my thoughts on writing and following God's direction. It makes me feel as if something significant is about to happen. When I acknowledge this feeling, I begin to doubt myself, and I feel arrogant for thinking I deserve something of importance in my life. I hear in my head, "Why do you think *you* are so special?" A small part of me believes I am not good enough for such a task, yet my heart tells me otherwise. I know the answer, but somehow I don't know...

12/08/08

Question: How do you tolerate suffering, both emotionally and physically?

Today is the Feast of Immaculate Conception. It is 12:44 pm, and I am sitting in the adoration chapel at St. Catherine of Sienna Church in Metairie, Louisiana. On this special day I pray with Mary, the mother of Jesus, and I ask her to assist me in obtaining courage, strength, knowledge, wisdom and discernment. It is amazing to think that not only did Mary hear Angel Gabriel's message that she would be conceiving the son of God, but that she actually believed it. Mary listened, understood, acknowledged and accepted the mission for which she had been chosen: living God's will, without doubt, no matter how unbelievable it appeared and no matter how crazy it sounded. She respected His word. I admire her for having the courage and obedience to believe the unfathomable.

I realize Mary is a blessing. Her life is an amazing example. Her strength seems unimaginable. While sitting in the chapel, I ask Mary, "How did you endure such great agony while watching your only Son be crucified?" I hear a very soft voice in my heart, "God. My Father." I am learning it is only through faith, trust and dependence on Him that we are carried. I want to learn more!

12/9/08

Prayer: Sweet Jesus, please teach me how to obtain
           unwavering trust and dependence on God and God
           alone.

This morning as I sit at the kitchen table drinking my coffee,
I meditate on an image of Jesus, and I ask Him to assist me in
obtaining unwavering trust and dependence on God and God alone.
I say this prayer from the bottom of my heart with all of the
strength I have within me. I know if I can accomplish this great
challenge, I will have the tools to successfully navigate through
life. I certainly hope for the best, but I want to be prepared for the
worst.

My father is the perfect example of facing adversity with
courage. He suffered a massive cerebral hemorrhage on February
16, 2008. He was sixty-three years old at the time. By medical
standards he should be dead, and it is only by the grace of God and
his excellent health prior to this incident that he managed to
survive.

Prior to this incident, my dad was consistently active. He
exercised daily and had the physique most twenty-year-olds would
envy. He flew planes frequently, hunted by horseback, skied
challenging slopes, ventured into scuba diving, leisurely played
golf, swung a tennis racquet, and he absolutely loved to be center
stage singing and dancing at parties. Being the motivator he was,
he would gather my three brothers and I together drilling us to be
leaders in life.

Unfortunately on this day, his life turned full circle. Our
leader would now need to depend on us as he struggled to recover
from this devastating blow. Today, he has gained movement on his
left side although his right side is still paralyzed. Speaking is very

difficult for him; he knows what he would like to say, but more than often he can't find the power to translate his thoughts into speech.

I pray to God, and I ask Him to supply us with His strength. Our hearts ache for my dad and our feet are weary, but we are not beaten.

12/10/08

Discovery: Listen, learn, watch and see.

My sweet, younger brother, Michael, purchased a ticket for me to attend the Metairie Country Club Christmas luncheon with his wife, Tereza. I was overwhelmed with busy work, and it was the last place I thought I should be going. I had a quick, little conversation, asking Jesus what I should do. I heard His excited, yet firm response from within, "Go!" I respond, "Okay! Okay! I wanted to get out of going, but when You speak, I am learning to listen!" I trust Him enough to know that He has His reasons; it could be an opportunity to meet someone, learn something, or simply listen to someone share an experience. I love to discover purpose!

Dressing quickly, I threw on my favorite grey pencil skirt, a high-collared, crisp white shirt draped with a long necklace, black high heels and a black clutch. I thought, "Maybe Jesus wants me to see the production of a fashion show?" I have been working on developing a line of jewelry in hopes of also sponsoring a foundation that would be fed by a percentage of the sales. I could optimize on two things that I love: designing and helping others. I pray about the jewelry often, hoping it is not a distraction, but rather a dream to be fulfilled.

En route to the luncheon, I began telling Tereza and our friend, Marie, about the jewelry I'd started creating and how excited I was about the vision. Upon reaching our destination at Saks Fifth Avenue, we checked in at the front desk for our table assignment. I immediately noticed large tables displaying a beautiful jewelry line that would be featured at today's Christmas luncheon! I smile and think, "How not ironic, Jesus!" The guest speaker, Joan Hornig, is the designer. She is beautiful, smart, sharp and undeniably inspiring. She spoke of her success on Wall Street and a promise she had made to give back. Her promise was to match the amount of money she had once made. She spoke of the importance of philanthropy and how she started her jewelry line on her dining room table. Today, she contributes 100 percent of her sales to the charity of the buyer's choice. Wow! I was completely inspired by her words *and* by her actions. This is what Sweet Jesus wanted me to see and hear. How cool to know I recognized His nudge! I listened, and followed His direction so He could teach me through others.

As the valet pulled my car around the corner, I smiled and slid into the driver's seat. I paused, looked at the image of Jesus that stands next to the speedometer, and I thanked Him for encouraging me to go to the luncheon. My phone alarm, which is set for 3:00 p.m. daily, a powerful prayer time, went off at that very instant. Again, this was confirmation He had sent me to listen, to learn, to watch and to see—one day, this will be me.

12/12/08

Practice: "For we walk by faith, not by sight." 2 Corinthians 5:7

My youngest brother, Christopher, whom we call, "Critter," just called to tell me our dad had cried uncontrollably last night. He was trying to communicate his frustration in his very broken and damaged voice, uttering words of disappointment, discouragement and anger. Our dad, the motivational speaker, needed to be reminded of the words and actions he taught us.

Wanting to encourage him, I searched through a multitude of photo boxes at my parent's home. I found several pictures of him dancing, singing and laughing on stage at a Christmas party. I showed him the images, and we started laughing. He was smiling as he gazed at the photos, whispering to me in his raspy voice, "I miss that." I made him slowly repeat after me, "I will walk! I will talk!" We said it over and over again. I reminded him that he must keep his faith.

To continue the pep rally, my mom arranged a dinner with some of their special friends in an effort to boost his spirit. Being the fashion coordinator that I have always been, I volunteered to dress my father for their date. I grazed through his closet and pulled out his stylish blue jeans, a white button down shirt, a black cashmere sweater, a camel cashmere sport coat, his shiny, black shoes and his large watch that shines brightly. We laughed as I struggled to get him dressed, and my attempt to get him back into the wheelchair was very rough considering my petite stature and his large frame. At that point, he laughed even harder with an expression on his face that screamed, "Oh my God, help me!" We laughed hysterically as I sarcastically said, "Well, at least I have you looking good!"

My mom, who is the ultimate optimist, constantly exudes a positive and loving spirit. Even after a long, hard day, she enthusiastically dressed for the evening and came down the stairs bubbly and smiling. As usual, she looked beautiful, and she was ready to have fun. When she saw my dad, she exclaimed with excitement, "Dave, this is the old you!" She lovingly hugged and kissed him, saying how handsome he looked. They were both happy, and they literally rolled out of the front door: my dad in his wheelchair and my mom joyfully pushing him from behind. I smiled as I watched them. It was a reminder of what a true partnership exemplifies: contagious love, energy and enthusiasm, no matter what the circumstances are. I am blessed to be a witness and to learn from their actions.

Thirty minutes later, I received a phone call from my mother crying hysterically from the back of an ambulance. Immediately after arriving at the restaurant to meet their friends, my father began to have what appeared to be a seizure. He was non-responsive, and they were en route to the hospital. My joy and optimism were shattered in an instant. I frantically jumped in the car with my brother, Michael. This would be the first of several seizures that he would experience from the trauma he suffered from his cerebral hemorrhage.

My daily mantra is one of the very few Bible verses I can recite by memory. It is short, simple and to the point: 2 Corinthians 5:7, "For we walk by faith, not by sight." I repeat the verse to myself daily, and it slowly finds a way into my heart. In life, our vision and our perspective are so limited because we can only see what is *literally* right in front of us. Daily events can lead to stress, worry, grief, despair and feelings of hopelessness. We all experience this at times. Today, as these overwhelming, hopeless thoughts poison my mind, I literally stop them from entering my soul, and I speak out loud, "I know I can't overcome this situation, but with God, I can!" I repeat this until hope returns. I remind myself that my ways are not God's ways. His solution is always better than my solution. I remain at peace knowing my life is in His loving and protecting hands. I have forced myself to accept and embrace difficulty, knowing that I can grow from every challenge if I so choose. I view this as an accomplishment, accepting His way, the better way, even when I don't understand why.

12/13/08

"MAY HIS NAME BE GLORIFIED AND HIS HEART AND LOVE FELT BY ALL. MY PEACE I BRING, MY PEACE I GIVE TO ALL."

My wise, eight-year-old daughter, Susan, told me to look outside at the full moon. She innocently said, "Mom, if you make a wish on the moon, it will come true." I watched her as she sat in the kitchen chair, closed her eyes tightly and silently made a wish. I wondered what she could be wishing for...

I decided to follow her lead. I was very tempted to ask for something shallow that I wanted, until I quickly remembered what I needed: fulfilling my goal of complete and total dependence on God and God alone. I realized that with this one wish, all of my dreams will come true—that with this one accomplishment, I would actually be granted countless wishes. I gazed out of the window. I stared at the big, bright moon glowing in the sky. I closed my eyes and said, "I wish for complete trust and dependence on God and God alone." In that moment, I realized all of my dreams were about to come true. I whispered to Jesus, "I wish for my heart to be true to You. For if You ask, I promise to do." He responded, "May His name be glorified and His heart and love felt by all. My peace I bring, My peace I give to all."

12/14/08

"THIS IS THE TRIATHLON OF LIFE THAT YOU ARE TRAINING FOR. YOU NEED ENDURANCE, ADAPTABILITY, DISCIPLINE AND FOCUS."

I had a great run at Pontiff Park yesterday morning. Running gives me great clarity, and I hear my coach's encouraging words, pushing me to my greatest potential, "Slow and steady. We are going for distance. If you start out too fast, you are going to burn out quickly." Of course, I feel so charged and enthusiastic I can't help but pick up my pace. My excitement and energy start to get ahead of me. When this happens, I overwhelm myself and tire. I hear Him say, "You see, what just happened? You started out too fast, and you are burning out. Remember, you are focusing on distance, not speed. This is the triathlon of life you are training for. You need endurance, adaptability, discipline and focus. Remember, your burden is light. Look at Me, I am carrying your cross. I just need for you to stay focused on Me and stay in motion." A vision came to my heart. I see my coach, and He is close to my age, handsome, physically fit, but yet not too muscular. His medium-length hair is pulled back loosely, and He is wearing long, navy blue Nike shorts and a white, sleeveless t-shirt. He carries a large cross behind His back with ease. As I start to feel tired, I ask Him, "Jesus, how did you manage the pain and torment during your crucifixion?" He responds naturally and without hesitation, "My mind was with My Father." I mull over His response as we continue running and every so often He interjects reminders to me. An example is when my mind begins to wander into the future, and I hear Him sternly say, "Where are you?" I smile coyly as I know I have been caught in my thoughts! I reluctantly respond, "Too far out." He asks me, "Where are you supposed to be?" I answer with a smirk on my face, "Right here, with You." He asks, "What happens when you are in tomorrow?" I answer, "I lose today." "That's right!" He says, "Keep your focus right here, right now. Stay in motion. I will do all of the work. I just need for you to stay in motion." As we continue to run, I respond, "Got it!" My iPod is jamming, and I am running with ease. In my heart, I hear a strong but gentle voice speak slowly, "Yoooou are looooking goooooood today. Keep uppppp the good work." I look into the sky, knowing He is somewhere, and I thank God for His encouraging words. I continue to run in the sun with a smile on my face as I follow Jesus.

12/15/08

Praise: I thank God for sending Sweet Jesus my way so He can teach me a better and more peaceful way of living.

I absolutely love the morning because I find tremendous beauty, peace and clarity in silence. I have been waking up at 5:00 am for years. When I was a young mother, it gave me the time to soak up a moment of solitude before my precious baby girls would wake and start the day. Once they were grown, I continued to wake up early so I could get a jump-start on my growing interior design business. With piping hot coffee in hand, design books and magazines at my side, my beloved white MacBook stares right back at me. This is what I considered to be the peaceful start to my day…working feverishly, trying to get in as much as possible before my two daughters, Susan and Sophia, quietly meander into my home office with their silky blankets, pillows, "lambie," crazy hair and the sweet smell of their morning breath that only a parent can appreciate and enjoy. A big smile would be plastered on my face as I rose from my desk chair and collected them on the sofa. My hugs and kisses smother them as I snuggle and say, "Good morning, little angels!"

It was after this innocent, sweet and brief, yet, cherished moment that I would go into autopilot. I was the Energizer bunny that kept going, and going, and going, moving furiously in all ways. My heart would catapult into a race while I juggled making breakfast, lunches for school, coaching tired girls to get dressed, making up beds, fixing hair, cleaning the kitchen, dressing myself and planning my day, "Gym? No gym? Meeting? No meeting? Calendar, paperwork, cell phone, purse, protein drink, bottled water, book bags, lunchboxes, show-n-tell, ready?" I lived in a rush against time. Pause.

I take a deep breath, and I thank God for helping me. I thank God for sending Sweet Jesus my way so He could teach me a better and more peaceful way of living. Little did I know He was doing a major renovation on me. Yes, the interior designer was being renovated. No, not renovated. Gutted! He saw that a new design was desperately needed.

This particular "project" was screaming out for help. God had the perspective to see beyond what was in front of His eyes: a stylish young mother living in a beautiful house, a successful interior designer driving around town in a nice car and appearing to others as if she was living the American dream. What He did see made Him sad. He saw inside this young lady. She had no direction, and she genuinely thought she was doing everything that she was "supposed" to do.. She thought she would find peace through her house and the surroundings. She thought her success was measured by a growing bank account. She thought the ultimate luxury in life was being able to provide the luxuries of life. She thought she was responsible for "fixing" people, when in fact, the person she needed to fix was herself. On top of it all, she was literally broken from a failing marriage. God knew her heart was ready to meet the challenge. He saw that regardless of her circumstances, she had hope and she prayed her heart out to Him every night. She genuinely believed God could show her the way. He knew this girl survived on faith, and she wanted to be all that He created her to be, if only she knew how. Her heart ached and her soul was begging to be set free. This girl was me.

12/16/08

Question: Do you really trust in God?

Exactly one year ago, my life changed. December 16, 2007, I was living in Houston, Texas at the time. Life as I knew it stopped, and this is when my renovation began. I would like to start off by noting that prior to my dad's cerebral hemorrhage my mom would often tell me, "Your father and I have been holding our hands together in prayer as we ask God to bring you and your brothers closer to Him. We want all of you to have peace and release the stress you hold in your lives." I was appreciative of their prayer, and I thanked her, but I did not really understand her request to God. I thought I was fine.

I was raised Catholic, and I have always had a heart that longed for God. What I didn't realize was that I was fighting Him on the most critical element: control. Control is lack of trust, and I would have never thought that I did not trust in God because I pray to Him every single night! I always thank God for the day he has given me and for all of the blessings in life. I pray for the sick to be healed, for the lost to be found and I always beg Him to lead me down the right path, although, I often chose otherwise. This being the case, how could I think that I trusted Him?

Fortunately, my dad called me on this very day. He knew I was going through a very difficult time in my marriage, and he wanted to check on me. We spoke on the phone for a good forty-five minutes, which is very unusual. Although we talk often, we rarely talk during the day because everyone in my family is too busy working. I have three brothers, and we are all very competitive. Needless to say, during our conversation he offered me his support in whatever decision I made in regards to possibly filing for a divorce. He was careful in that he would not advise me on what I should do, but rather, he only offered his support by telling me how much he loved me and that he is proud that I am his daughter. As we were about to hang up the phone, he quickly interjected one last note, "I picked up a book at the airport called, Becoming A Better You by Joel Osteen, and I am really enjoying it. Why don't you buy a copy?" I responded, "I bought it two weeks ago at Kroger's while I was waiting in the checkout line with my groceries." My dad suggested, "Well, read it! It has a chapter or two on relationships, and it may do you some good." I always respected my father, and I agreed to his advice.

That night, I climbed into my big white bed holding a copy of Becoming A Better You. I pulled the covers up over my body, adjusted my pillows just right, and I started digging into it. I gained such wisdom from the words Joel Osteen had penned. I remember feeling pretty good about myself, thinking, "Good, good! I already do that. Great!" I was feeling confident until my hand S-L-O-W-L-Y turned to the chapter on stress and anxiety. Those two words started leaping off the page. It was as if I was watching a horror film, and the words would just expand and contract, expand and contract. I readjusted myself, needing to sit up more attentively as my eyes grew bigger, and my nose was now buried deep into the pages. Oh, my God, there it was: the key to my life that had been missing for all of these years! The answer was in that one sentence, "When you feel stress and anxiety in your life, YOU ARE NOT TRUSTING GOD."

What? I read it again, this time more carefully and more slowly, "YOU ARE NOT TRUSTING GOD." It literally felt like a stack of books had just been dropped on the top of my head. It hit me that hard! I immediately started apologizing to God, speaking out loud in conversation, telling Him how sorry I was, over and over and over again. I began crying. My heart was literally throbbing with pain, and my emotions came rushing out of my body. I was physically and emotionally worn out. I explained to God how I thought I was supposed to "fix" everything and everyone around me. I thought I was helping Him. I forcefully said, "God, You can have it all back because I can't do it anymore! I need You! I need Your help! I can't live with this pain anymore. Help! Help me!"

I was sobbing at this point, and I meant every single word I said. I spoke with such great strength, conviction and sincerity that you would have thought I was begging God for my last breath when suddenly, out of thin air and from across my bedroom, by far the most powerful and strong force rushed upon me. A "force" reached deep within my being, and it felt as if a super-sized commercial vacuum was sucking everything out of me. I was in a complete state of shock as my body went limp, and I suddenly felt as if I was a balloon that had just been deflated. My heart immediately slowed down, and I quickly had an unusually strong sense of peace and calm. I felt light and relaxed. The pressure was completely gone.

I sat in my bed not knowing whether I should be ecstatic or completely petrified. I rambled, "Oh my, God! God, was that You? Oh, my God. Oh, my God. I know it was You. Thank You. Oh, my God, Thank You! I am scared, but it is okay, I know it is You." All at once, I was extremely frightened yet trusting, confused yet enlightened, excited yet peaceful and light yet strong. I felt overwhelmingly loved, and I knew God heard my cry for help. He *literally* removed my anxiety and stress, and I could not believe how wonderful I felt inside. I thought for sure it would not last, and I said to Him, "Can this really be?" But, deep in my heart, I knew the truth.

At this point, I continued to read more as I was so full of excitement and had a new sense of wonder. I reached a point in the book where Joel was talking about the death of his father and how much pain his mother was feeling. He talked about his mother watching a red cardinal in her Houston home. He explained that every morning, at the same time, a red cardinal would appear in his mother's backyard, and she loved watching this bird. Eventually the cardinal disappeared, and she missed it so much because it had become part of her daily routine. One day, Joel went to his mother's home to pray with her and asked God to heal her pain. During their prayer, a red cardinal appeared in her backyard. It served as her reminder that God was with her.

I was so touched by this story, and for some reason, I knew the red cardinal would have significant meaning to me. To be honest, I didn't even really care about birds. It was just this intuition, this feeling that said, "Pay attention." While confirming this thought in my mind, I had the chills, followed by goose bumps, even though I was not the least bit cold. I said out loud, "God, I don't know anything about red cardinals, but I know You are trying to tell me something. I don't know what it is, but it is something!" I was almost giddy at this point. So much had happened in one night, and now all of the sudden, I was receiving "messages" from God? I thought again, "What is going on? Am I dreaming? Is this for real?" But once again, my heart knew the truth.

The next morning, I woke up with the same sense of peace and calm. I spoke out loud, "God, I am about to put You to the test and see if I remain at peace today. Here I go." The girls were waking up, routine was kicking in, and I was smiling. I was so excited because I was passing the inner peace test! No elevated heartbeat. No anxiety was setting in. I was calm, and I was moving slow and steady. I exclaimed, "OH, MY GOD! YOU ARE GOOD!" I could not believe the difference in how I felt. I drove the girls to school, and I went to The Houstonian to work out at the gym.

After I finished lifting weights, I thought about how amazing it is to walk in peace. As I was about to head back home and get to work, I stopped myself as I recalled the advice my brother, Michael, had given me. He said, "You know, you really need to start walking or running. I think you would really enjoy being outside. It is so relaxing." I looked at my watch, and I was tempted to go to work until I thought about the miracle I received the night before, the restoration of inner peace. I recalled my promise to God, to live my life in a new, balanced and trusting way, HIS way.

I immediately changed directions. I walked away from the parking lot and headed down a new trail. I turned on my iPod, and I started walking. I was simply admiring the beautiful sunrays splitting and beaming down between the multitude of trees, and I began to reflect on my experience from the night before, still feeling shock and disbelief. I gazed up at the tree just ahead of me, and low and behold, there it was. A red cardinal was perched peacefully on a tree branch directly in front of me! Immediately, tears began rolling down my face and once again, my body was full of goose bumps and chills. Crying softly, I spoke from within, "God, as crazy as this experience may sound, I knew it was You last night. Thank You for the confirmation and for showing me that You can reveal Your presence in such a simple way. Thank You for my new, peaceful life. I love You with all of my heart."

This was just the beginning.

12/18/08

"YOU ARE TO WORK SMARTER, NOT HARDER. SMARTER. NOT HARDER."

As I was getting dressed yesterday morning, my mind accelerated into the future. I quickly heard my Coach's sweet voice interject, "Today I want your thoughts on Me. When your mind begins to wonder, bring it back to Me immediately." I smirked. Jesus caught my thoughts, as usual. I responded with a frustrated sigh, "Got it."

Several times throughout the day my mind continued to blast into the future. Jesus would immediately catch me and ask, "What are you feeling right now?" I answered, "My jaw is starting to tighten, and I feel tension." He asked, "What were you just thinking about?" Every single time, my thoughts were fixed on future concerns. Jesus spoke so sweetly and patiently, "Do you see what makes you anxious? Relax. Stay in the moment. Speak My name and focus on Me." I responded by speaking out loud, over and over again, "Jesus, Jesus, Jesus, my mind and my heart are with You. You are my focus. You are my goal." As I focused on Jesus, my mind and thoughts eventually relaxed, and my peace was eventually restored. I realized He doesn't miss one thing, and His gentle and sweet reminders are expressions of His love and concern for me.

I am completely blown away by the power of His Spirit. I feel so overwhelmingly loved. I can truly feel the inside of my chest expand in His warmth, and it wraps itself completely around me, always bringing tears of joy to my eyes. I think to myself, "My God, I want those who do not know You to feel what I feel inside. I want the lost and lonely to feel Your amazing love and peace. Furthermore, I want You to receive the love You deserve. Please tell me, show me, how I can help You?"

As I am writing this entry, my mother and sister-in-law, Stephanie, are laughing at me. I stop writing, and ask, "What is so funny?" They begin re-capping the events of last night. After a family dinner, I suggested we all take a break and not work until after the new year. My dad gave me a thumbs up, laughing and whispering in his broken voice, "Sounds good to me." My mom, smiling, spoke up, "Yes, let's relax and enjoy the season. Let's have fun!" We were all excited about the plan! I made everyone promise to keep their word. Of course, my three brothers were not in on this conversation, but hey, three out of six is better than none. Stephanie and my mom began laughing even harder and could barely speak. Between complete fits of laughter, Stephanie said, "Katie, who would have thought you would be walking around with a bird sitting on your shoulder (that would be "Princess" Susan and Sophia's parakeet), preaching peace, love and Jesus, relaxing and telling everyone to take a break from working!" Tears started to stream down my face, but this time, the tears came from laughing so hard! I thought, "Yes, this is me!" Then I quickly thought, "Ohhhhh, myyyyyyyy God! Whaaaaaaat has He done to me?" I try to continue writing, but I am still laughing! I realize my "before and after" picture is drastically different. In my heart, I hear God laughing with me, and He says smiling, "Only, Jesus!" He then asks me with enthusiasm in His voice, "What was one of our missions?" I immediately smile, and I remember what Jesus told me, "You are to work smarter, not harder. Smarter, not harder." This is one of the daily mantra's that He would have me repeat as I would run through the park, light on my feet, body in motion and my eyes locked forward on Jesus carrying my cross.

Smarter. Not harder.

12/19/08

Prayer: Sweet Jesus, I pray for humanity to not only open up
their hearts, but to open up their mind to the reality that
God does exist...in a very personal and fun way.

Today, I am writing in the adoration chapel at St. Catherine's. It is
a place that I have truly come to adore. The peace, the clarity, the
silence is all so beautiful to me. I sit in the very back row and just,
aaaggghhhhh, r-e-l-a-x. Everything becomes so clear.

I had never been to an adoration chapel until this past
summer. It was on my "to-do" list, but I just couldn't quite make it
happen. One day, a dear friend of my parents, who is very spiritual
and who has been a mentor of mine, called me. She said she
received a "message" while she was praying. I was to go to the St.
Catherine's adoration chapel. She told me, "Katie, I don't know
why, but for whatever it's worth, I want you to know. It was
specific in that it is St. Catherine's." I trust Shannon and her
spiritual authenticity. I am learning how to understand "messages,"
and I knew I was being "called." This was the push that I needed to
get out of my comfort zone. It was time for me to take action and
do something that I typically would not have interest in. It was an
opportunity to trust the direction God was showing me.

That same week, I did as I was told. It was the beginning of a
great blessing. It was the discovery of my peaceful hideaway! I
was so pleasantly surprised to experience the beauty of sitting in
silence with the Blessed Mother, praising Jesus in the Tabernacle.
I thought to myself, "What an honor to be in such high presence.
I feel like I am part of a royal court!" I enjoyed it so much that
I continued to visit regularly, as a "visiting" adorer. Every time
I would sign in at the entrance of the chapel, I would see a bulletin
board with a sign that read, "Committed adorer needed."

I pretended like this message was not speaking to me, although I knew it was. I just kind of brushed over it. I thought, "Ohhhhhhh, noooooo, Jesus! I did not just hear You tell me to 'commit,' and I would walk away with a guilty feeling sitting in my heart. I would try to justify my reasoning: 'I am too busy already! I don't need to add another obligation to my life. I will just come as I please, as time permits.'" Well, that worked for a short time, until one day, a sweet, elderly lady approached me. She spoke in a whisper trying not to break the silence in the chapel, "Excuse me. One of our committed adorers has not shown up today, and I must leave. The Blessed Sacrament (which is the host, the body of Christ) can't be left alone. Can you substitute for me until the next adorer arrives?" I answered enthusiastically, "Of course, no problem at all." We smiled at each other, she thanked me and she left the chapel. Within five minutes she was back, and she was tapping me on the shoulder. I turned to look up at her, and she had a form in her hand. She asked me quietly, "Will you sign up to be a committed adorer?" My God! I will tell you, He will get you when He wants you! My "pretending" to not hear Him was not going to work this time. I looked at her precious face smiling back at me as she patiently waited for my response. Lord, she resembled Mother Teresa! He knew I could not say "no" to her! Well, the rest is history. And, once again, God always knows best.

So I say again, "What a blessing!" It is a great gift that was given to me. I am so thankful I have learned how to hear His voice and to have the ability to communicate with Him on such a deep, personal and intimate level, not to mention, fun!

My thought and prayer today is this: it is my wish that humanity open their hearts and open their minds to the reality God exists in a very personal way, and that He is waiting to speak to you. Give Him the chance to finish what He started. Allow Him to show you what He can do for you. His promise is not to escape hardships, but rather to guide you through them and teach you how to learn from them. And, finally, to experience just how humorous He really can be!

12/20/08

Lesson: My success is directly related to my dependence on God and in fulfilling His purpose designed specifically for me.

Who would have thought that self-reliance could actually be detrimental to your success? Aren't we taught to be independent and strong? As many love to say, "Look out for number one." and "Cash is king." If I would have listened to my own thoughts or famous quotes just as these, I would not be successful. This is when I am thankful for free will. It was by choice I decided not to listen to my ego, but rather to the truth that God placed in my heart. I recognize my success is directly related to my dependence on God and in fulfilling His purpose designed specifically for me. It is my faith and hope that feeds my soul, nurtures my dreams and fans the blazing flame burning inside me.

I now have freedom and true success. I am independent and I am strong, but only through my dependence on God. He is my number one. He is my king.

12/22/08

YOU NEED TO HAVE ADAPTABILITY. DO NOT GET
COMFORTABLE RUNNING THE SAME PATH. LIFE IS NOT
A CONSTANT, BUT RATHER EVER-CHANGING.

I received another message the night before last. The words were spoken very simply and there was no explanation. I heard, "Direction. Management. Mobility. Endurance." As I woke, I found myself slowly repeating the words. I understood it to be the tools required to fulfill my purpose, and I had an understanding that Jesus would provide direction and management, but my life partner would also assist us. The words "mobility" and "endurance" were meant directly for me. Mobility meant I would be in more than one place and traveling often. Endurance would be required. The journey that I will be embarking on requires great effort and flexibility on my part. I was told, "You are not to fear."

As I write this morning, I am reminded of one of our runs last week. Jesus said, "You need to have adaptability. Do not get too comfortable running the same path. Life is not a constant, but rather ever-changing." When I was approaching my first mile marker, I heard Him say, "Change directions." I immediately turned around and started running in the opposite direction. I know He sensed that I was wondering why I was doing this, and He said, "Never get used to life being the same. Watch how different the same mile feels when you run in the opposite direction. Your perspective will change. It looks different, yet it is the same. Embrace change. Embrace the path you are on no matter how uncomfortable it is. When your heart and mind are open, you embrace instead of fight. You remain peaceful." I listened carefully and continued to run. When I hit mile marker number two, he interjected, "Again, change!" I immediately changed directions again, and He tells me, "Do you see? You are changing directions, but you are also staying in motion. You are not stopping. Keep your focus on Me and always stay in motion." Suddenly, my mind flashes to a recurring dream. I am running in a very long race, and I am close to the finish line. I am tired, yet I still have energy. The spectators are angels and saints, and they are cheering me on in a sea of puffy, white clouds. It is beautiful and sunny. My surroundings are swarmed with souls jumping up and down in excitement. They are all loudly calling out my name. I am completely fulfilled, smiling so bright, and my arms are raised high above my head as I carry the most beautiful trophy I have ever seen. My trophy is Jesus.

12/24/08

Challenge: Refuse to allow doubt, outside influence and the opinions of others to override the truth in your heart.

Christmas Eve. When I stop and silence myself to reflect on this miraculous day, so many thoughts run through my mind. I try to imagine what Mary and Joseph must have been feeling. The anticipation so great, the responsibility unimaginable, the fear of the unknown and the labor of love they had both been carrying, so innocent and pure.

I know if I had been Mary, my thoughts would have been, "Can this really be? Did I hear the message clearly? Could I be mistaken? Why me?" But yet, you know the truth in what you have been told, no matter how unbelievable it appears to be. The truth only grows stronger in your heart, leaving no room for doubt. Your mind denies you the right to believe something so magnificent could possibly happen to you, but your heart is overruling your mind. Which do you choose to believe in, your mind or your heart? I am learning to listen to my heart. This is where my faith takes root. It is a feeling so grand that it can't be stopped. It begs and pulls at your soul so hard you eventually become powerless. You surrender your thoughts and allow your heart to guide your dreams to reality.

I imagine this to be a small part of what Mary and Joseph did. Refusing to allow doubt, outside influence and opinions of others to override the truth in their hearts. They had the strongest form of trust that mankind can have with God. Complete and total surrender.

I pray for that trust. I pray for confidence in God and faith so strong that no matter how hard the wind blows, my feet remain planted in the heart of God. Never breaking. Only growing. Only loving.

Today, I thank Mary and Joseph for remaining steadfast in their mission and in their promise to God—for listening, understanding, believing and for never giving up. May we all follow your beautiful example.

12/25/08

Lesson: Do not allow your mind to limit your actual ability to endure a long journey.

Happy birthday, Sweet Jesus! What a beautiful day to celebrate.

Mary lived in the moment and truly surrendered her life to God. I believe this is the only way she survived such a great mission. If she tried to control her life, she would have been overcome by fear. Her mind would have limited her actual ability to endure her long and strenuous journey. Fortunately, she utilized God's wisdom and drew on His strength by finding favor in her heart. She simply trusted God.

12/26/08

WILL YOU HELP ME?

I wake up this morning with my coffee and my standard supplies, which consist of *Jesus Calling* by Sara Young, my Bible, my notebook and the *Devotion to the Divine Mercy*. On the cover of *Devotion to Divine Mercy* is an image of Jesus, and it radiates peace, serenity and love. I also stand a small prayer card of the Blessed Mother, Mary, next to this and keep several special saints cards in my book. This is what I use for meditation. It is my visual reminder of my "team" and the Spirit that is with me at all times.

I was intrigued the first time I saw the cover, *Handbook of Devotion to Divine Mercy* from revelations given to Saint Faustina. On the cover, Jesus's image is powerful, and I focus on His piercing eyes because through them I see genuine love, honesty and compassion. Across the top of the book it reads, "Will you help Me?" I feel strongly, in my heart, that Jesus just asked me for my help. I think to myself, "Are you kidding me? Me, help You? How can I help You?"

12/27/08

WRITE. SPEAK.

God continually encourages me to write. It is a very strong message that my heart has been receiving for over a year. It is simply spoken, "Write." Followed by, "Speak." I question this request because I have never had the desire to do either one of these things, nor do I have the experience. I ask Him, "Write? I am not a writer. Speak? Speaking is essentially teaching, and I am not qualified. I can't imagine either one of these being a recommendation? Are You serious?" Regardless, I am being taught to listen to the voice in my heart and not to the voice in my head. I question God further, "I really don't understand. What am I suppose to write about? Interior design? My life? This just can't be? I am simply a girl who loves to design. I do love communicating with Jesus in Spirit, and I am completely fascinated with the mystery of spirituality, but I am not seasoned or educated with facts, dates and the history of the church or the Bible. I am not a statistical person who rattles off information. I am the person who only speaks in confidence through experience; I am a relationship type of person. I do trust You, and I know what I am being told, but it sounds completely ridiculous to me."

I decide to follow His advice and give it a try. I start writing about my life, starting from childhood. It does not feel right at all, and I tear up the pages in frustration. This continues over a period of time. I continue to pray, and I ask Jesus again in total confusion, "Please, help me! What am I suppose to write about?" I meditate on that thought, and I sit in silence, waiting with my pen in my hand. A thought I know is not my own, gently sweeps through me, and I slowly and peacefully write down what is planted in my heart, "You are to journal Our journey." I knew at that moment, without a doubt, this is His answer to me. It sounds easy enough. I will simply write about all of our interactions, the directions I feel His Spirit prompting my soul and the actions I take. It will be similar to an experiment. I will document my experience of complete surrender and trust in God and the results (or lack there of) that follow. What is the reality of spirituality? Where will He take me?

12/28/08

WHISPERING WORDS OF WISDOM, LET IT BE, LET IT BE.

Why are relationships complicated when they should be quite simple? I write about this subject as I am in the midst of a divorce. I think to myself, "Who am I to talk about this subject?" Looking back, I can honestly say that I am so grateful my life played out as it did. I have absolutely no regrets. I am blessed in many ways, although I can promise you I did not feel this way during my personal storms. But, now, I can see it all so clearly. It is actually quite beautiful. Only God has the ability to make something that was challenging into something meaningful. You see this is what I mean when I speak of God's confirmation. Just as I wrote that last sentence my iPhone began to ring, and "pop" there is a picture of my two beautiful daughters that appears on the screen. They are calling me from their father's house to wish me a good night and tell me they love me. It is my reminder that with God, joy can come from pain. It all depends on how you view your circumstances. Perspective. It is one of the words that is "sent" to me continuously, and now, it is my saving grace.

I have learned how to look and observe circumstances, arguments and relationships from a different perspective (not my own) as a way to understand and recognize how we each justify our belief and actions. When we learn how to respect another person's perspective and hold love above all else, confrontation can end, and understanding and resolution can begin.

I sit in silence. I relish in feeling this amazing inner peace. I am in complete thanksgiving, and I thank God for His help. Suddenly, out of nowhere, I hear in my heart, "Whispering words of wisdom. Let it be, let it be." Although my intuition tells me

Jesus has just planted these words in my heart, my mind questions my intuition, "Where did that come from?" I begin to reason with myself: I know that was not my own thought! I never listen to The Beatles, nor have I heard this song in a very, very, very long time. Nothing has triggered that verse. This is just too random. That could not be my own thought. Jesus, I know it is You! What does that mean? What are You trying to tell me?

I know this message has great significance to me, but I have no idea why. Later that day, I tell my mother what I heard Jesus communicate to me. I ask her if she knows what He could have meant? She replies, "I have no idea. If I were you, I would just pay attention."

I literally can't stop thinking about it. "Whispering words of wisdom, let it be, let it be."

12/29/08

Challenge: Utilize the gifts that God has given to you. Share your
gifts with others. Enjoy!

Last night, I thought about the consultation I had with a face-
reading expert. A client of mine was so generous in treating me to
a fabulous retreat to Cal-A-Vie, an amazing spa and resort located
in California, which is where I met Barbara Roberts in February
2007.

Barbara was the guest speaker one evening. She is a
professional face reader who consults with the FBI, national news
groups and has speaking engagements at a countless number of
seminars. She was offering private consultations, and I thought it
would be very interesting to see how well she could "read" me. Let
me say, her accuracy amazed me! She taped our thirty-minute
consultation, and when she finished, she gave the tape to me for
safekeeping.

Something that night urged me to listen to the tape (this is
what I know to be the presence/voice of the Holy Spirit). I did not
really remember what she had specifically said to me, although I
do remember her precision in what she revealed. I began to search
through my files to locate it. Soon enough, I found it. It had never
even been rewound. I scrambled to find a tape player, crawled up
in my bed, pressed the rewind button and pressed play. What I
heard her say for the second time was more amazing than what I
initially heard. Remember, she knew nothing about me. This is
what the recording captured "When I see you, a scripture from the
Bible comes to me referencing two or more being gathered in my
name." She continues to tell me my spirituality is very important to
me. She says I am Catholic with a traditional religious background,
and I am opening up for my faith to be broader and more personal.

My relationship with God is deep and devotional. My spirituality is authentic. I am tolerant of people who are not as spiritual because I have a concept and a sense that people do their best with what they are given. I have tremendous tolerance. I love people. People trust me and are drawn to me. My focus is on my family, which is very important. I am a survivor. I am shy, patient, loving and sweet, but I am also solid. I may sway in the wind, but I do not fall. There is steel in my principles, but I am soft as a flower when kindness is needed.

She tells me that I love what I do. I have great taste in material objects, art, fabric, texture, wallpaper and interior design. Aside from my creativity, I go beyond the glamour of it all. I enjoy most, matching people's personality to décor and objects so they feel relaxed and healed. It is the core that I am after—bringing out the best in them through their environment. My love and appreciation of beauty is very strong by nature, which is an aspect of God. God is beauty.

My fascination with flowers, colors and fabrics started as a young child. I am a perfectionist who hates making mistakes, especially if it hurts someone. But if I do hurt someone, I make amends, and apologize, and I try to repair it. It is difficult for me to let go. I am high-spirited, self-employed and I love to travel. I like to be given information about what to do. I take it and work from the inside out to present it. My love of music is strong. It is a form of healing and meditation. I use it to increase my mood and bring joy. I like to listen to it while driving. When I have too much stress in my life, it comes out in the form of digestive issues. The problem leads to not being able to digest and absorb what I consume. I tend to over give, and I need to learn to use discrimination in this area. There are things I need to give to God. My greatest and strongest attributes are my big heart and my artistic ability. These are my gifts.

I thank God for encouraging me to listen to this tape. It is a gift to know my design talents are utilizing the gifts God has given me. I pray I continue to use them to the best of my ability. I pray that others will enjoy them as well.

I think back to a message I wrote down in my journal while I was reflecting on my jewelry line. My heart spoke these words,

"Wear the accessories, but furnish your soul with spiritual necessities." Hopefully, my designs will be a visual reminder of peaceful living, classic simplicity, elegance, style and love of the soul and Spirit.

12/31/08

Lesson:　　Praying to God is not the same as living through God.

I try to encourage my three brothers to open up their hearts and minds for a deeper understanding and relationship with God. They all have different personalities, and they tell me how they pray at night. But I am all too familiar with that old routine, knowing that praying to God is *not* the same as *living through God*.

1/2/09

Challenge: Live in the pursuit of God.

Although 2008 was by far one of the most difficult years thus far, it was also full of blessings and miracles. I have learned and grown, both personally and spiritually, that I feel like I am bursting at the seams. I have an unusually strong hunger and thirst for life. I want experience so I am living in pursuit of God, knowing He will direct me to the greatest level of excitement, adventure and mystery. I want to explore His trail, and continue on the journey of a lifetime!

1/3/09

KNOW THAT I WILL BE SENDING SOMEONE VERY SPECIAL YOUR WAY.

I went to my "treatment" yesterday, that is my session at the adoration chapel. I once heard, Kitty Cleveland, a beautiful singer with a spiritual soul compare adoration to a radiation treatment. It struck a chord with me. I realized how I had been battling a cancer of my own. The cancer was my old thoughts, but I am being radiated with God's love and truth. I know the other visitors must wonder about me. Without fail, I am the girl sitting in the very back row, under St. Catherine's mural, crying and drying my tears with tissue. I know the other adorers must think I am experiencing something tragic in my life, when really, I am experiencing true love and joy. The tears that rush down my face burn with love. It is my reminder of Jesus's eternal river of grace and mercy upon us all.

I hear a calm, strong voice speaking very clearly and with great precision. It is an overview of His plan for me. God told me it was similar to playing football, and He has assigned me the position of the quarterback. I am to receive directions from my coach, Jesus, and act on His direction by throwing passes to the appointed team members. He said I would be doing several different tasks simultaneously, but I would not feel the weight of the load if I follow His direction. He continued, "First and foremost, you are to be a mother to your children. A sacrifice of time is to be expected, but the quality should not be compromised. The time with them should be focused, loving and fun, which, in the end is more memorable. Wake in the morning, focus on Me, and write in your journal. Balance exercise and stay healthy. Volunteer at the children's school, but in a simple way. Do not overcommit yourself. Continue your interior design jobs with clients during the day. Evenings are to be spent having dinner as a family, discussing the day, telling stories and sharing love and laughter. Routine, discipline, respect and prayer are essential. Once the children are settled in bed, relax and get a good night of sleep. You may work on the jewelry line in your spare time, as you please. I will stop at this because I do not want to overwhelm you. I know how fragile you are. Know that I will be sending someone very special your way." I immediately perked up and thought, "What? Who? When? Where?" His only response to my question, "Time." He then continued on by thanking me, telling me that He loved me and that I was doing a beautiful job. He ended on a light note by saying very amusingly, "Hang in there, kid. The world is waiting for you." The way He said it made me smile and laugh because it was not spoken in a way that I thought I would hear God. It was so very casual. I sat in the chapel confused and questioning His words. I began reflecting on what was just spoken to me. My thought was: "What was that about? Did God really just say that to me? Maybe that was my own egotistical thought? But then again, I don't even speak in that manner?" Deep in my heart, I knew the truth.

Lightning literally just struck outside of my window, and a very loud thunder rolled just as I was finishing the previous sentence. I interpret the perfect timing of the thunderous roar to be confirmation that God is speaking to me, revealing Himself in the sky, as I write about *our* dance.

1/4/09

Lesson: Listen to the "voice" that comes through your "speakers." Tune in and reach your destination.

As I've mentioned, I'm working on a jewelry line. Over the summer, a family friend, referred me to a local jeweler she knew well. I called him, and he was very kind and helpful on the phone. He gave me direction and a few contacts for assistance in bringing my vision to reality. My cousin, Judy, referred me to Baldwin Taylor for jewelry supplies and accessories. I thought it would be a starting point. I pulled up to the store and I walked in straight towards the side counter. The large gentleman sitting behind the counter was busy at work. I excused myself and asked him if he could help me. He slowly picked his head up from his paperwork and looked me squarely in the face. I politely introduced myself, and I went on to tell him I was looking for a craftsman to make prototypes for a jewelry line I was working on. I further explained I wanted someone who was a "one-stop shop." He told me he knew the perfect person for me. He said, "His name is John. He's been around for years, and he is full of wisdom and insight. He can do everything for you." I was so excited. I smiled and politely asked for his phone number.

I called John on January 2, 2009. We scheduled a meeting at his home on January 3, 2009 at 11:00 a.m. He lived not far from my home, but I wasn't quite sure how to get there. I utilized my favorite feature on my car, ON STAR navigation. All I have to do is simply press a button, speak and—voila—a voice comes through my speakers and tells me exactly how to get there. I can't help but compare it to how Jesus instructs me. It's similar in that you don't know the roads ahead, but you have the confidence in knowing that it will bring you to your destination. It feels uncomfortable driving blindly, but you feel relief and excitement when you arrive exactly where you need to be.

I arrive at John's house, and it is a tiny, old cottage that appears to be a mess. There was a dog barking behind the chain link fence. I was slightly intimidated, but John was standing there waving his arms, signaling me to come inside. I slowly grabbed my folder of ideas and hesitantly got out of my car. He led me to the back of his house where a little, old shack was standing. I entered cautiously and followed him to his desk where he pulled out an old, dirty office chair for me to sit in. I slowly eased into the seat. I began sharing my ideas with him, and the entire time I spoke, he just sat silently as he looked at me expressionless. Regardless of how uncomfortable I felt, I continued to explain to him that I am very spiritual and my desire for this particular project is to express my passion for God, Jesus, Mary and all of the Heavenly Hosts in a modern and fresh way. Slowly, he swiveled around in his chair. A flaming torch was burning behind him, and he reached out for something. Quietly he said, "I have been working on this for someone. Is this what you mean?" He passed a medal to me, and there He was. It was a beautiful, vintage inspired medal of Jesus's face. John said, "Or something like this?" and he whipped out a necklace that had been buried under his white, ribbed tank top. It was a large medal of the Blessed Mother. All I could do was gasp and say, "Oh my God."

John's shop turned out to be a little hidden treasure chest. He was so knowledgeable, wise and unique. He taught me so much more than just the basics of jewelry making. He gave me a new and interesting perspective on life, people and religion. He reminded me that I could not save the world, but what I could do is to stand firm in my endeavor. After a two-hour conversation, rain began to sprinkle and I thanked John for his time. Right before I walked out of the door he said, "I have to ask you something. Why do you wear a man's watch?" I smiled, and in a serious but sarcastic tone, I responded, "I may be a small girl, but I have big shoes to fill. Besides, I like the weight of it on my arm. It feels good to me." He nodded his head with acceptance and said poignantly, "You know, many teachers wear men's watches."

I told him that was a very interesting comment, and I scurried out of the door trying to beat the rain.

For the remainder of the day, I thought about John's advice and our conversation. I think it was a conversation driven by God, as I believe He can advise us through others. I felt, once again, that He was helping me. Teacher? Hmmmmmmm…

1/5/09

ONE DAY AT A TIME. YOU CAN REST EASY IN MY PRESENCE.

This morning I am having that bad, sinking feeling. Self-doubt loves to try to seep back into my mind. It loves to haunt me. It is a constant battle, and I must turn my thoughts around right now before the poison kills the truth in my soul. Pause. With God anything is possible, and nothing is too difficult. He is with me. He is guiding me. I have nothing to fear. I remember His words, "One day at a time. You can rest easy in My presence." I need to repeat His words over and over again. I need to allow Him to penetrate my mind, and replace the self-doubt that found its way in. Pause.

Songs often randomly sing to my heart. I just heard Peter Gabriel's song, "Don't give up…when times are getting rough, you can fall back on us, oh, please, don't give up…" A female with a soft, gentle and peaceful voice sings the chorus. It reminds me of the voice of an angel. She is singing the song to me…

1/9/09

Lesson: Prayer and meditation increased my ability to focus.

As I sat at my desk yesterday, I was surprised to see how efficiently I was working. In the past, I thought I had attention deficit disorder and a doctor suggested I try taking medication. I did as she suggested, but I felt wired, compulsive, and I could not sleep. This was not the solution for me. To my surprise, it's prayer and meditation that has increased my ability to focus. My mind has been trained to stay in the present, and focus on the tasks at hand. I was fielding calls from clients, volunteering for cafeteria duty at my daughters' school, scheduling the girls' doctors appointments, speaking briefly to friends, picking up the children from school, working on design projects, responding to e-mails and overseeing Susan and Sophia with their homework. I never lost my patience, I maintained my inner peace, I focused, and I completed the tasks I had set out for the day. I feel good! I know I can do this. I will continue to practice so my balance remains steady, and practice eventually turns into habit.

1/12/09

Lesson: Gifts from God are talents that come to you naturally, but they still require time, work, development and patience.

I went to the jewelry and gem show at the Pontchartrain Center in New Orleans yesterday. I pulled into a parking spot, took my picture of Jesus off of the dashboard, and placed Him in my pocket. As I was walking through the crowded parking lot I could not help but notice all of the Texas license plates. I was thinking about how I'm currently living in New Orleans, yet I am still surrounded by Texans! I should have known Texas would be in my blood. In college, everyone always assumed I was from Texas. I found it interesting, and I always wondered why. Obviously, they all knew something that I was oblivious to…

I purchased my $8.00 ticket, filled out a form and headed inside. I found myself feeling like a fish out of water. I had absolutely no idea what I was doing or looking for. It was sensory overload! I took a deep breath and decided to just observe and see what was out there. I began collecting business cards from vendors that I found interesting, but soon enough, I started feeling completely overwhelmed and confused as to how I was going to pull this off. My infamous doubt began creeping back in my mind, and I had to fight it off. I began reciting my favorite mantra in my head, "For I walk by faith, not by sight," over and over again until I relaxed. Finally, I finished looking at all of the vendors, and I left the center mentally exhausted. I couldn't wait to get out of there!

As I drove back home, all I could think about was how challenging the jewelry is going to be and how easy and natural interior design is to me. I began to sympathize with the clients that approach me. Their feelings of being overwhelmed and feeling clueless as to how to pull their home together made me realize how much they depend on me to pull their ideas and dreams into a reality. For me, interior design is as simple as breathing, but I know, in order to broaden my gift, I must embrace being uncomfortable and face the new challenges ahead of me.

1/17/09

Practice: Turn disappointment into, "Jesus, I trust in You."

Surprise, I'm in Texas! I'm sitting in my comfortable bed at The Houstonian Hotel, sipping my coffee, looking out of the big, beautiful window and staring into the trees.

It brings me back to the time in my life when I was struggling and fighting to find inner peace and freedom in my life. As I reflect, I can still see myself walking through the wooded trails with my iPod singing words of inspiration. I can feel the tears rolling down my face, stinging my cheeks into a rosy shade of pink. I would walk with determination and flooding thoughts of wanting more, wanting to break free but yet feeling totally vulnerable, sad and insecure. With these conflicting feelings raging inside of me, I would hear a Yusuf Islam song play, and it became my dance, my reminder of why I was going to fight, find courage, overcome fear and break through the chains that bound me. How fitting, the song is titled "Heaven, Where True Love Goes." "I go where true love goes, I go where true love goes, and if you walk alone, and if you lose your way, don't forget the one who gave you this today. Follow true love, follow true love...and if the storm should come, and if you face a wave, that may be the chance for you to be saved. And if you make it through the trouble and the pain that may be the chance for you to know his name..." and as the song plays the fighter in me comes out swinging. I wipe away the tears of pain and my chest begins to swell with warmth, and my steps turn into long, powerful strides. Not only do I want to give love, but also I want to receive love. Loving until it hurts so beautifully. Once again, knowing He is holding my hand, guiding me and giving me His love and support, I quickly turn my disappointment into, "Jesus, I trust in you."

1/18/09

NEVER TAKE THE SHORT CUT.

Saturday morning, I relaxed in my hotel room, ate my Cheerios and geared up for a run in Memorial Park. I bent down to tie my new Nike running shoes, and I felt ready to go. It was a beautiful day, and the temperature was a perfect, mid-sixty degrees. I parked on North Picnic Lane and walked onto the track, stretched my legs and body before I began to run at a nice, steady pace. I was looking at all of the walkers and runners, thinking about how interesting it was to see so many people, all varying in many different heights, shapes and sizes. I think it is beautiful, interesting and such a great testament to life—to see individuality! All of us, human beings, living and breathing with the same blood flow, yet we each have a different build, a unique purpose, a unique style, and when it is mixed together, it adds such an interesting blend of diversity, adding energetic creativity to the world. I begin to question. Why do some people want to be the same as someone else? Why do some people think their way to life is the only way to life? Why are some people looked down upon if they live life in a non-traditional manner? Don't misunderstand me, I have some traditional views, but who am I to judge others?

I continue running and discover a shortcut. At that very moment, my beloved coach, J.C. (Jesus Christ), interjects, "Never take the shortcut." I immediately understood I had to take the long road home. There are no shortcuts in life. It is only with time, patience and endurance that we successfully accomplish our goals. I realized that no matter how tempting it looked, the easy way is not the right way. This message is to be applied to all areas of my life. My new way of living: taking my time, being thorough, meditating, asking the Holy Spirit for discernment and guidance, utilizing my knowledge and then, hopefully, making a wise choice. I joke with God frequently by saying, "Can You move any slower? This is taking a long time!" I hear Him say, laughing back at me, "Patience, my dear, paaaaaatience." I answer Him back, "I know! I know! You are all about timing and precision, not speed. You have to orchestrate many things in order to make it just right!" He answers me back, still laughing, "Myyyyyyy, you are a slow learner!" I smile and quietly laugh to myself at His fun and humorous remark! In that moment, I think about how much I completely adore God, and I continue to run joyfully—as I take the long way home.

1/19/09

Praise: Sweet Jesus, thank You for always making Your presence known to me, for comforting me in my darkest moments, and for giving me the precious gift of faith in God.

As I drove back to New Orleans yesterday after meeting with clients in Houston, I could not help but feel a mix of emotions. Houston is a city I came to love and embrace. For all of the newness, I found excitement, energy and kindness in people. The big city, the bright lights and the fast pace are all very much a part of who I am. I thrive on the style, the fashion and the buzz around town. But, there is the other half of me that thrives on being grounded in simplicity and ease, which is what New Orleans offers me. It is literally a fishbowl that holds my precious family, friends, a unique flavor and spice for life, food, flair, spirituality and strong faith. The Saints (our football team) disappoint us time and time again, yet it is our faith, our hope and our dream that one day, we will have a winning team!

I am filled with confusion as to where it is I belong. I need Houston for contacts and business, yet I love New Orleans. Mired in that thought, I glance down at my dashboard, and I catch the sparkle in the eyes of Jesus. His eyes speak to me, "Trust in Me." Although the circumstances and dynamics throughout the day change, I can trust that there is always one constant in my life, one Being that will never change, one Spirit that will love me for all of my gifts and for all of my failures. I thank Jesus for always making His presence known to me, for comforting me in my darkest thoughts, and for giving me the precious gift of faith in God.

Reflecting on my trip to Houston, I realize not everything I had hoped for came to fruition. I was hoping to make more contacts for work and to get a feel for what single life will be like. I need new jobs in order to be more financially stable, and after speaking to several of my single friends—they made the dating scene sound like doom and gloom. To be honest, they made it sound awful! I think to myself, "Well, it sounds like it will take me years to meet the right man. Oh well, I will just work and enjoy time with my daughters, friends and family. One day it will happen." I take a deep breath, and I push out a sigh of relief. I look at Jesus on my dashboard, and I grin from ear to ear as I say, "Although I'm disappointed in my trip, I trust in You! I know Your ways are always better than mine!"

1/23/09

Question: Jesus, when is someone going to help me? I am tired. The journey has been long. I am overwhelmed. I am ready to receive. My eyes are open, my arms are open and my heart is open. Please, Jesus, speak to me! HERE, I AM, WAITING.

My spirit was down today. I can't stand when my apparent circumstances get the best of me! My mind told me that I deserved a pity party. Unfortunately, I fell prey, and I sulked at my desk from 10:00 a.m. to 12:45 p.m. I did not accomplish one thing other than to commiserate with myself and complain to Jesus, "All I do is give, give, give! When is someone going to help me? Lord, have mercy on me! I have pure intentions and my heart loves human beings. I spend more time wanting to help others than I do working on my job that is needed to support my family. Where is that person who has my same heart, my same pure, genuine love? Someone who wants to help me, without expecting anything in return? I am ready to receive! My eyes are open, my arms are open and my heart is open. Please, Jesus, speak to me!" He responds softly, "Here, I am. Waiting."

I hear God's voice in my heart, and He sounds somber and fatherly—He reminds me, once again, "Dependence on Me and Me alone."

He is my "someone"! *He* is my source! *He* is my help! I ask myself, "Why do I fail to believe in His power in *all* things?" I finally begin to understand—by me having a shortage of money, resources and a partner in life, I will recognize the glory in His work, therefore gaining confidence and trust in Him. He wants to show me that He will provide everything I need. I need to rely on Him for success and happiness, not others.

1/26/09

Challenge: Put your thoughts and words into ACTION.

Jesus tells me my new challenge is to put my thoughts and words into action. I am able to visualize it, think it, speak it, but I must work on living it. Now, this is where I need a push. Help me, J.C.!

1/28/09

"Sweet Little J of mine, I want to help You shine!"

My daughter's school had a special mass yesterday. The focus was to let your light shine. The light is a gift from God, your talent. "Will you hide it behind the bushel tree or will you let it shine for all to see?"

As the mass closed, the students began to sing, "Oh, this little light of mine, I'm gonna' let it shine, let it shine, let it shine…" As the song continued to play, my daughter, Sophia, turned to me and whispered, "Mommy, why do you call Jesus, Sweet J?" I responded, smiling, "For me, a nickname is personal, and Mommy's relationship with Jesus is very personal. It's playful and fun to speak sweetly to someone you love so much." She smiled at me and started singing hew own words to the tune, "Sweet, Little J of mine, I want to help You shine, help You shine, help You shine…"

My prayers are being answered.

1/29/09

Meditate: Perspective." Look not to what is seen, but to what is unseen. What is seen is transitory, what is unseen is eternal."

–Corinthians 4:18

I know it's difficult to trust in someone who isn't physically present. It brings my heart to one of the very few Bible verses I know, "Look not to what is seen, but to what is unseen. What is seen is transitory, what is unseen is eternal" (Corinthians 4:18) In other words, embrace the challenge and reap the reward.

1/31/09

Direction: For me, there is only one way, one path to take, and it is God's Way.

In my dream last night, I was flying in an airplane, the door was open, and I was looking out into the great wide open. The view was so overwhelmingly large and absolutely beautiful! My attention was drawn to a map—it was being presented as a means of assisting me in navigating my path. I noticed it immediately, my destination was at the very bottom of the map, and it was the only road that I wanted to travel. When I found it, I exclaimed with great excitement, "Oh my! Look! There it is! There is a path called 'God's Way!' That is so cool that someone named a road after God. That is where I want to go! Take me there!" God's Way was at the very bottom of a very large mountain. The other roads appeared to be easy, fun and colorful, and there were so many different options to choose. Regardless of the other alternatives, I was only interested in one road: God's Way.

I was dropped off at the bottom of God's Way, and it was the most beautiful, sunny day. The temperature was perfect! I had on my hiking clothes—short khaki cargo shorts, a white ribbed tank top, Nike running shoes and my sport sunglasses. I was walking up the mountain with ease with my bottled water in hand. I was so amazed at everything in my presence—I loved it! As I hiked up, there was a steady stream of gloomy looking animals slowly coming down the mountain. I watched them closely, and I wondered, "What happened to them? Why are they so sad?"

On my hike, a gentleman was accompanying me for safety, although I didn't know who he was, nor could I see his face. He watched me closely from behind, allowing me to make my own choices, but also offering me direction and teaching me life lessons as we walked.

This morning, as I reflect on the meaning of my dream, it is so clear to me. My journey has just begun, and I am at the bottom, slowly making my way up a large mountain. God is with me. The animals were representing human beings from all different walks of life. These particular beings were carrying heavy hearts, carrying feelings of loss and giving into defeat. Their road had been long, and they were weary. These individuals were not utilizing God's grace and power. There was no other way for them, but down.

As for me, I was happily, effortlessly and peacefully walking. I am enjoying my journey, embracing every moment, and learning from the school of life. I had found God, and I was allowing Him to guide me, and I am slowly making my way up the mountain. For me, there is only one path to take and it is "God's Way."

2/1/09

Lesson: The more I remove myself from a situation, the more I see things happen. My way only interferes with God's Way.

As I was running yesterday, I was reflecting on everything that transpired last year. From a professional standpoint, I realized my true love and passion is my desire to inspire others to simply live their life through God, and in doing so, your talents and gifts are revealed and utilized. In return, you fulfill your destiny. In April, 2008, after reading my interview with *domino* magazine, my mother told me, "You are going to have the *domino* effect on people." I started laughing at her comment, thinking that was absurd, but my mother quickly stopped me and said, "I am serious. You will have the *domino* effect on people." As ridiculous as I thought it was at the time, I now pray she's right. What a beautiful gift that would be!

I have been blessed with the gift of faith. Faith in God defends me in any battle that comes my way. The more I remove myself from a situation the more I see things happen. My way only interferes with God's Way.

2/9/09

Believe: No meeting is by chance. Timing is everything. Seize every moment, every connection and every opportunity that is placed before you.

I have been working in Houston for the past few days. A fun and fashionable local publication, *Papercity*, is featuring a house I designed. It happens to be the home of a dear friend of mine. I believe the photographs will translate the family's life style which is colorful and fun.

I always enjoy being in the company of the magazine's features editor, Laurann Claridge, and I owe *Papercity* a lot for giving my work the opportunity to be featured on their pages. In September 2007, they featured my personal home. From that photo shoot, I met an extremely talented photographer, Tria Giovan—she is based in New York and is one of the most sought after photographers in the field. Her work is published in everything from *Veranda*, *Southern Accents*, *House Beautiful*, *Travel and Leisure* and more. Our photo session was a success, and we exchanged business cards, vowing to stay in touch. Several months later, Tria contacted me and asked if she could submit the photos of my house for possible publication in another magazine. *domino* was one of the publications, and that is how I ended up as a "*domino* 10." Once I was featured in *domino*, other publications and editors began contacting me. They were looking for more of my work to publish. The cycle had begun. It is my reminder that no meeting is by chance. Timing is everything. Seize every moment, every connection and every opportunity that is placed before you. You never know what door God may open...

2/13/09

I NEVER CLOSE A DOOR WITHOUT OPENING ANOTHER. THE DOOR TO YOUR FUTURE IS WIDE OPEN. COME INSIDE, AND ENJOY THE RIDE. YOU WILL BE DELIGHTED WHEN YOU SEE WHAT'S INSIDE.

My youngest brother, Christopher, and his wife, Stephanie, live in New Orleans, Louisiana. We have been renovating their house, and after fifteen months it's finally complete. The three of us made a great team. It was a great collaboration—Stephanie was the ultimate researcher, and Christopher was a great sounding board for me, offering great ideas and insight. I had the vision to see beyond the devastation that Hurricane Katrina had left behind. We all took the project to heart, and it was a labor of love. The features of the home that are most unique, and add the most charm were the most difficult elements to work with. I wanted to incorporate reclaimed French antique stone around the front exterior door to add some history, character and depth. Not one person agreed with me—everyone said it was going to look terrible, including the architect. Regardless, I stood firm in my opinion, and we proceeded. It took the installers several attempts to get it right, but my intuition and my vision saw perfection in the end. I thank Sweet Jesus for giving me the confidence to trust my instinct. Otherwise, I would have given in to everyone else's opinion. I would have written off something that is so beautiful and unique. The prayer card we placed in-between the stones that create the surround make it even more special. It is a card with a picture of Jesus standing under a very similar stone surround. On the back is a prayer, a blessing for the home! We all gathered around, holding hands and prayed the prayer to Jesus. I knew He was standing guard and watching over all of us. We were choked up and teary eyed at the realization that one journey was ending, but a new one was just beginning.

Simultaneously, I was working on the renovation and construction of one house, while I was living through the destruction of another house, my own. The tears, the pain and the heartache were felt daily, yet I remained at peace. I found many reasons to smile.

There is nothing pleasant about divorce, and no matter how hurtful the circumstances are, I have never stopped loving and praying for the man I married. I could feel his pain just as much as I felt my own. It is very difficult to let go of the past, no matter what the situation is. It becomes a part of you and a part of your history. Letting go is losing a place in time that was once familiar to you, painful or not.

I hear Sweet Jesus whisper to me after I just wrote that last sentence, "I never close a door without opening another. The door to your future is wide open. Come inside and enjoy the ride. You will be delighted when you see what's inside. Your future is big, and bold, and bright for you never lost sight of My guiding light."

2/19/09

I WILL TAKE CARE OF YOU. I WILL TAKE OF YOU. I WILL TAKE CARE OF YOU.

Yesterday was difficult. My circumstances, as I saw them, began to overwhelm me. Again, I repeat, "as I saw them." This is when I like to say, "The eyes of sight are so defying." Seeing only what is literally in front of you limits your mind, causing you to see too many impossibilities. Sight is simply too short.

My sight was only allowing me to see my father in a wheelchair, my mother changing his diaper, the economy negatively affecting my work, my bank account dwindling to nothing, selling my possessions to pay off debt and a messy divorce still lingering six months past what should have been the finalization date. Let's just say that my short sight and my mind were getting the best of me.

After dropping my daughters off at school, I drove back home with fatigue—I was thinking only of the worst possible outcome in all of my challenges. I start praying to Jesus or I should say, complaining to Him. I was telling Him how tired I am, and that I am truly depending on Him to help me through this difficult time. Suddenly, I begin to hear Him slowly repeat, "I will take care of you. I will take care of you. I will take care of you." Although, in my heart, I knew it was Jesus speaking to me, my mind said, "You are just making this up. You are trying to tell yourself what you need to hear so you feel better. Is Jesus really speaking to you?" I suddenly became filled with doubt, and negative energy came rushing forcefully upon me. I feel weak and sick with my circumstances in this very moment, and my doubts continue to rage upon me. Literally, not even one minute later, I see a car pull up next to me. I glance over, and I immediately get the biggest smile on my face as I burst out into a joyous laughter. The driver next to me has an old, beat up car—it is being driven slowly by a cute, old, black man who looks like he hasn't a care in the world. His car is literally covered in Jesus bumper stickers, and I mean literally! The stickers are everywhere, with only a few exceptions, the windows! You could barely see the maroon paint job peeking through the mass of stickers. It was the funniest car I've ever seen, and the driver was so darn cute on top of it! For me, it was confirmation from Sweet Jesus, in His perfect timing, and in His humorous and fun way saying, "Hellllllloooooo! I am *with you*! It is Me *talking to you*! Good morning, from Jesus! Relax! Smile!" Lord, He knew I needed a good, hard laugh and a sign to boost my confidence in Him, a sign to confirm our language of love. He then spoke to me, "Do not be afraid. I am *always* with you." I began to cry tears of love, comfort and joy. Joy in knowing that He cares, and that He loves me just as much as I love Him. Joy in knowing that I live in Spirit, and that even Jesus can be funny!

When I got home, I began to tell my parents what had just happened. As I did, the church bells from St. Francis began to ring loudly. Once again, it was perfect timing, my confirmation—Jesus has me covered, literally!

2/20/09

Action: Love your life!

My happiest moment yesterday: I pulled up to my parent's home after picking my daughters up from school, and we were gathering all of their book bags and projects from the day. Out from nowhere, Sophia exclaims with great excitement and joy, arms open wide and her head held high, "I love my life!" That is music to my ears, warmth to my heart and a treasure that you simply can't buy. Love life! Amen!

2/21/09

I LOVE YOU!

I was reflecting on the amazing renovation on my soul. I feel so glorious, and I want others to have this experience because it is so unbelievably powerful, beautiful and peaceful! It is a feeling that words will never be able to describe.

I thought about what makes my experience with Jesus so personal and successful. The first word that sprang to my heart was "awareness." I had the knowledge that Jesus was with me in Spirit, but I did not know how to "feel" Him, "hear" Him or "see" Him. I thought it was sad and wasteful that Jesus sacrificed His life for humanity, yet I didn't know how to optimize and utilize His Spirit. I found it too difficult to trust in someone that I only had knowledge of. What I needed was *awareness* in learning how to experience His Spirit. I know my learning style well enough to realize that a textbook, the Bible or a classroom setting would not teach me as much as my senses would. I decided to start placing a picture of Jesus in all of the places that were a constant for me. I needed a "visual" reminder that He is with me all day, everywhere I go, and that His Spirit resides in the present tense, not in the past. I meditated on His sweet image whenever I sat down at the kitchen table to pray, on the dashboard in the car while I would drive, in my bathroom where I would get dressed and at my desk where I work. Unknowingly, I was slowly learning how to be aware of His presence.

In time, video messages suddenly began to appear in my soul, simply out of nowhere. The scenes are so authentic, that I began to see the reality of His Spirit. I also began to feel His presence. A thought, not of my own, would come to me, and I would acknowledge to Jesus that I recognize His Spirit prompting my soul. In return, the air would become full, and a warm rush would reach deep within my being, filling me up with an amazing sense of love, peace and euphoria. I translated the timing of this action to be His Spirit communicating to me, and showing me love. The feeling is so strong that it takes my breath away, and my emotions are stirred deeper than I ever thought possible. It is my belief that Jesus, knowing my needs, would infuse the scenes within my soul so I could humanize His Spirit, which would help me relate to Him more easily. Before this realization, I felt doubt because I did not know how to connect with Jesus, in Spirit.

When I saw my father in ICU on the brink of death, I felt Jesus's presence next to me. His arm was around me, and He whispered, "He will be okay. Not now, but in time." When I was confused and broken in my marriage, I sat at my desk crying uncontrollably. I pleaded with God to give me an answer. I asked Him, "What am I supposed to do?" He responded slowly, with authority in His voice, and simply said, "Love."

I had just moved back to New Orleans from Houston after separating from my husband. I was sad about the failed relationship, and I was walking aimlessly through my parents family room when I heard, "She Will Be Loved" by Maroon 5 playing in the background. As the words sang to my heart, all of a sudden, with the eyes of my soul, I saw an image of Jesus. He was standing outside of my parent's home, waiting on the curb of the street, dressed in His white robe. His hair was wet, as it had been flattened by the rain, and there was no expression on His face. I could see He was sad, full of concern and sorrow. I stood there looking back at Him, experiencing my own sadness, and our eyes locked, but we were still standing at a distance. He spoke no words. He just stood there waiting for me. He had been waiting for a very long time. The time was right. He knew I was ready. I slowly started walking towards Him; it was as if the walk was in slow motion. As I approached Him, He started to slowly lift up His arms, and I walked directly into Him. He wrapped his arms around me, and I wrapped mine around Him. We held each other tight, in silence, and my face rested wearily on His chest. He gently and innocently kissed the top of my head, and the rain continued to fall on us. We finally stood as One.

His Spirit continued to grace my soul now that I was open to receive Him. One day, as I walked out of the side door to go for a run in the park I saw Jesus waiting outside for me again. He would wait patiently at the foot of the driveway, never wanting to intrude. I would smile back at Him with sheer joy. I delighted myself in knowing that His Spirit is present, and that He is patiently waiting on me. This time He was dressed in running clothes—His hair was loosely pulled back, and He had a big smile plastered on His face. I greeted Him with a full heart, open arms and a sweet, friendly hug.

Then, I began to hear Him, as I would wake in the morning. On occasion, I would want to press my snooze button because I felt crippled with fatigue, but instantly, with that thought, I would hear Him say, "When you want to quit that means get up and get going." My body would react automatically, and I would pop out of bed. When I would get too serious and discouraged, I would see Him break out into a Justin Timberlake-style of dance. Get a visual of that! My frown would immediately break into a smile and my belly was thrown into a fit of laughter. When I would burst out into tears and cry with a heavy and weary heart, I would see Him approach me with a warm and loving embrace. He would hold me tightly and whisper softly, "I love you." Once my savings account was depleted, I started selling my possessions due to financial hardships—I was practically down to nothing when I heard Him say, "Don't worry. The treasures you have found are everlasting." When I asked Jesus, "How can I help You?" He responded, "Follow Me and live My Father's will." I replied, "I don't know— what is His will?" He gently said, "Listen to your heart, it never lies." I responded with exhaustion, "How do I trust what my heart is saying?" Jesus then told me, "I will fill it with your greatest desires." And, this is how our rhythm began...it was so easy to follow, in + love, with Jesus.

2/24/09

FOLLOW MY LEAD. TOGETHER, WE CAN MAKE THINGS HAPPEN.

I walked out of the side door to head outside for a run. I was feeling great, and I stretched while the sun was beaming down on me. It warmed my soul. As a result, my mouth upturned into a great big smile. I took in a deep breath, exhaled and relaxed my body. Jesus was standing at the end of the driveway, waiting for me as usual. I slowly walked towards Him, excited as always. He looked back at me smiling, "How are you feeling today?" I answer happily, "Really good!" He said, "We are taking a different path today. We are running the streets." I respond, "That's fine." But in my mind, I was wondering why, as we typically run in the park. Immediately, J.C. responds to my inner thought, "You are ready. The streets are unpredictable. You do not know what lies ahead, but you have been trained well. Always remember what I have taught you—follow My lead. Together, we can make things happen." I nod my head in agreement, and we start our run. Jesus is always ahead of me, running effortlessly. Every now and then He glances back at me lovingly, keeping me in His sight while He softly sings tunes. Often, He sings strongly and highlights words of wisdom that I am to pay attention to. I simply follow...in+love.

3/3/09

Action: Surround yourself in love.

I accidentally deleted my address book on both my iPhone and my MacBook while syncing them. Uuughhhh! I literally began to cry because I lost all of my personal and professional contacts, e-mails, phone numbers and addresses. Unfortunately, I did not have my computer backed up. After feeling very sorry for myself, I finally dried my tears, took a deep breath and thought, "Jesus, what is the message?" I heard, "It is time for you to start all over."

Still distraught, but trusting in Jesus's wisdom, I began to say a prayer my sister-in-law's mother taught me to say repeatedly when you lose something that needs to be found. It goes like this: "Little Jesus of the lost and found, please help me find what I have lost, (your request goes here—mine was, "my contacts"). Amen."

I knew, in my heart, that Jesus wanted me surrounded by love, and He was going to bring certain people into my life. I would learn from them, and they, in turn, would learn from me. I have discovered that Jesus is always working in more than one way, bringing people together for a reason. I began to pray this sweet little prayer, over and over again, at every opportunity possible. Just as you might expect, my phone began to ring. People that I had not spoken to and that I had lost touch with from over a year ago began to call me from out of the blue. What I knew was *truth*. The truth in that Jesus was listening to my request, and He was responding, in His way—surrounding me in love.

3/5/09

SHARE YOUR LIFE WITH ME.

As I get situated at the table this morning, I hear Jesus speak in a happy and cute melody, "Good morning, Sunshine!" I smile, laughing at His address, and I say, "Good morning, Mr. Handsome!" I glance at Mary's sweet face next to His, "And, of course, Sweet Mother Mary!" I continue laughing at this very silly moment. Although I hear Jesus call me "Sunshine" quite often, I have never thought about why He calls me that until now. Well, as Mr. Mind Reader works, I hear Him quickly interject at my internal thought, "You are a ray of hope for those who are suffering. You are happiness, just like sunshine." I respond, "Well thank you, Jesus, but I still find it hard to believe that this is really happening to me." He answers, "Tell me why?" "I feel like there are so many wise and brilliantly trained scholars and professional holy people in this world. You know I am not scholarly, nor am I a history buff—names, numbers, dates and statistics will never be a part of who I am. My mind does not work like that." Jesus responds, "Which is exactly why you are perfect for this job. You break the mold. I know your intentions, and your intention is to genuinely love and to serve Me, My Father and My Family. You, journaling the details of our relationship, may not be based on biblical facts and scripture, but what you do offer is your whole heart, which is full of love for people. What you offer is a raw accounting of your intimate and personal relationship with Me. What you offer is reality. Do you know how happy you make Me by offering yourself fully to Me? You communicate with Me, and you share your deepest thoughts with Me. You are not trying to impress Me with facts, written prayers, reciting novenas and attending church, but rather, you are simply being you, in My presence. You want to share your life with Me. You share every thought, pure or not. You offer it to Me for advice. You accept your weaknesses—you embrace them, and you give them to Me. You rely on Me for strength, comfort, companionship, laughter, drying your tears, comforting your pain and yet, in the end, you are still smiling because you have the awareness, the knowledge and the wisdom to recognize that it is Me with you, loving you, holding you and whispering, I love you!" I begin to cry softly at His words and I say, "Thank you, Jesus. I love you. How could I ever live without Your precious Spirit?"

3/6/09

HOW CAN I HELP SOMEONE WHEN THE PROBLEM IS NOT OFFERED TO ME?

As I sit in the adoration chapel, I think about the frustration I feel when I work so hard, yet I don't see progress. I feel discouraged, and I begin to doubt everything I have learned. I feel in my heart what I know to be true, but what do I do when I want something that conflicts with God's commandments? I hear Jesus speak sweetly, yet firmly, "You obey. He knows what is best for you. You should know that by now. Maybe it's simply a matter of time. Maybe, it's not meant to be. Life is a daily struggle. Discipline takes time and proper training, learning how to resist temptations when they stare you in the eyes, living by law, doing what is right despite your own wishes, learning to live by God's will. This is trust!" Jesus continues, "Being honest not only with yourself, but also with Me is creating great teamwork. How can I help someone when the problem is not offered to Me? Again, this is a great example of choice. Your choice to come to Me for advice, knowing in your heart that My answer may not be what you want to hear—yet you still come to Me. Most importantly, not only do you ask Me for my advice and direction, you listen and you follow My direction, despite your own desires. This brings Me great joy! This is discipline! This is respect! This is trust! This is friendship! This is honesty! THIS IS LOVE! Thank you for sharing your most personal and intimate thoughts with Me. It takes courage to be so raw and vulnerable. Despite that, you still take a step forward, exposing everything inside of yourself for me to see, to touch and to heal. There is nothing left to hide. I love you! I love you! I love you!"

This is when I say, "Jesus, thank You for keeping me smiling!" My tears and sorrow quickly turn to joy.

3/9/09

Lesson: Doubt gains power when you place confidence in yourself and not in the power and glory of God.

This past weekend I was thinking, "How am I going to overcome my financial challenges in this economy? Doubt has set in. Frustrated with myself, I ask Jesus, "Why do I do this?" He answers, "You place confidence in yourself, not in Me." He is so right. Displaced trust.

I hear Jesus speak again, "Move on. Focus on what you did do. I saw beautiful things happen." He is right. Positive actions: I did start typing out my journal. Regardless of how insecure I feel about writing, I am confident in God's direction. I just hope I can do it well. Jesus speaks again, "Whom are you relying on when you just wrote that statement?" I answered, "Myself." He continues, "And...what did we just talk about?" I responded, "Placing my faith and trust in You." He says, "So, let's practice that today since you're having some trouble. Why are you having doubts? You say that you are confident in God's direction. This is contradictory." I reply, "I know it is. When I started typing, I began to think, 'Who is really going to find this interesting enough to read? This is ridiculous of me to think people will buy this memoir." Jesus responds, "First of all, look at what you just said, 'I started thinking.' Thinking is the problem. When you are thinking, you are only using your head, not your heart. Your heart loves writing, and your heart tells you this is a beautiful love story. You must follow these very simple rules. I know it is difficult for you, which is why you need Me. Let's work on nourishing you, and detaching you from other people's opinions. This is an example of where it is fitting—your concern is not how you feel. You love our story, our relationship and our journey. What frightens you is how others may *perceive you*. You must not listen to criticism. Focus on helping just one person, that person right now is you. The goal is to bring you closer to Me, for us to train together. If we can accomplish this, you have succeeded! Stay on course. You have come so far in a very short period of time. I am so proud of you. Keep up the great work and always remember, I LOVE YOU!"

3/11/09

Remember: You can't get what you want, until you know what
you want.

When I was lifting weights at the gym, Joe Jackson sang, "You
can't get what you want until you know what you want."

I believe the most difficult challenge for most people is
discovering what it is they want. Why? Knowing what you want
requires deep soul searching, contemplation, feeling, thought and
prayer. I think most people are too afraid to go that deep, afraid of
what they may discover, afraid that if their deepest desires don't
match their current role, they have to make a choice, to follow or
not to follow, to stay comfortable and complacent or to rise to the
challenge. I remember reading a quote. It said, "Whenever you are
comfortable, it is time to get uncomfortable." That statement is so
significant to me because it is so challenging. Life should be
constant growth, and growth requires change.

I challenge you all to get uncomfortable. Reach beyond what
is in front of you. Test your limits and stop living in complacency
by accepting what is unacceptable.

3/13/09

Question: Why would anyone think God is unwilling or unable to
open up a line of communication to all of us?

I see a Verizon Wireless billboard and it speaks to me. The
billboard features a group of professional men and women
standing together as a team. The tagline reads, "The Most Reliable
Network." Although I know this advertisement is for Verizon, I see
it as a reminder to me from my team of Heavenly Hosts—Jesus,
Mary, Joseph and all of the angels and saints—*they* are the most
reliable, wireless network. I must continue to have trust and faith
in all of them. I must communicate and trust in their promise to
work on my behalf, just as I try to work on their behalf. We are a
team. We are "wired" together, and the sky is the limit. I believe
heaven is re-programming me—this is not to say that I think I am
perfect or free from sin because I know that I am not! What I am
suggesting is that I am open to being "re-wired" by God.

I read a book called, *The Tipping Point* by Malcolm
Gladwell. It's an amazing book that investigates the factors and
reasons behind epidemics, trends and how little things can make a
big difference. While reading the book, I could not help but think
about "the fax effect, e-mail and Internet" The fax effect in
particular because the first fax machine that was ever made was the
result of millions of dollars of research and development, and it
cost about $2,000. But, it was worth nothing because there were no
other fax machines for it to communicate with. The second fax
machine made the first more valuable and so on...because fax
machines are linked into a network; each additional fax machine
increases the value of all the fax machines operating before it.
I know you are wondering where I am going with this comparison
and it is this: being linked to a network—God as the network,

increases in value when others operate before Him as well. You can create an entire network which would increase positive values and mindsets. Power and abundance come from value. The more people that have the software, the more people you add to your network, the more powerful it becomes.

I want to spread a "virus," a very contagious and healthy virus—a virus of hope, faith, trust and dependence on God. The more people it infects, the more powerful the epidemic. My goal is to reveal God's simplicity, and to create anticipation, not dread. I know from Malcolm Gladwell's study and from my own personal experience, that when you're overwhelmed with information people develop an immunity to traditional forms of communication, they turn elsewhere. I believe many people have an aversion to God because of the way God is preached. Preaching can be felt as forcing, speaking harshly, condemning and often I feel it can instill fear, as opposed to love. I want to be able to *relate* to God and His ways, not fear God and His ways. I believe the more you *know* God, the more you *respect* God. Love, loyalty and positive actions nurture respect. I believe that if people are aware of the simplicity, excitement and adventure of being in a relationship with God, it would be enlightening. Why not keep God simple? I assume people want real and meaningful relationships with friends, family and spouses—quality time spent together, good communication and expressions and actions of love. A relationship is a two-way street, which requires both giving and receiving. Why would God be an exception to the rule? Why not simply focus on nurturing your own, personal relationship with God—I believe everything else would fall into place.

3/21/09

Praise: Thank you, Sweet Jesus, for guiding my recovery.
TOGETHER, we won!

I woke from a dream and spoke aloud, "It is only because of You
that I made it this far." I was speaking to Jesus and Mary about the
love and peace they have brought into my life, and the realization
of the great importance of a healthy soul. In my dream, I was
crossing the finish line to my first journey—I was in a wheelchair,
smiling and pushing myself with my arms. I had lost all of my hair
and my ears were sticking out far from my head. I had been broken
down, I was left completely raw, and I was humbled. I was a
cancer survivor, only my cancer was my inner turmoil, my self-
doubt and my own thoughts breaking me down. Jesus guided my
recovery, and together we won.

3/22/09

YOU THINK TOO MUCH. STAY RELAXED IN BOTH MIND AND BODY. ALLOW MY SPIRIT TO FLOW THROUGH YOU.

I headed out of the door yesterday for a run—it was the most beautiful spring day! I paused, turned towards the sun, took a deep breath in and exhaled. I began stretching and thanking God for the beauty in this day. As I turned around, I realized I was being greeted by a young man wearing long, navy blue Nike shorts, a white sleeveless shirt, running shoes and a bandana wrapped around his head. I greeted Him with a big smile, "Hello! I love the do-rag, You are stylin' today!" Jesus smiled back at me, "I am glad you like it. I thought you would!" We began to laugh at our fun interaction, and as he continued to smile He asked, "Are you ready?" I responded with excitement, "Absolutely!" We walked, side by side, heading up the railroad tracks and down to the first block. As soon as we hit Falcon Street, we instinctively turned to the left and started running together. Nothing was said as we ran in sync. I started to think about something, and Jesus quickly interjected, "You think too much. Stay relaxed in both mind and body. Allow My Spirit to flow through you." I consciously stopped my thought, relaxed my upper body, and I took in a deep breath. We continue running the streets, and my heart turned to how fortunate I am to be following such a strong Man. Every move He makes is so graceful and effortless. I feel a love that is so genuine, and I rejoice at the thought of our partnership. I love watching this Gentleman as He carries the cross for me. It is beautiful to know that He loves me just as much as I love Him. He speaks, "Whatever you do, stay in motion. You are not allowed to stop." Although we are running, I know he is referring to our journey. I assure Jesus, "I promise to do everything I can. I will not stop."

Throughout the duration of our run He continues to interject every so often, but in a more stern voice than usual, "You are not allowed to stop. Do not be afraid." With these words spoken in a serious tone, I understand them to be commands from God. Orders I choose to follow. I have made a promise to God and to myself.

As we approach the end of our run, we slow down the pace and walk to cool down. While trying to catch my breath I say, "Jesus, I feel tired." He responds casually, as He looks back at me, "Do you want a lift?" I smile and exclaim, "Absolutely!" He stops and He slightly bends His knees far down enough for me to jump on His back like a child. I jump up, and I hug Him tightly as I rest my head on the back of His shoulder. I tell Him in a sincere voice, "I love You so much." And He responds lovingly, "I love you too." In this childish moment, I jokingly say, "I am so sorry about all of the prickle's on my legs. I did not shave." He answers me, smiling through His laughter, "Are you kidding me? This is nothing. Remember, I wore a crown of thorns!" We both laugh, in + love, as He carries me home.

3/24/09

"VIVA LA VIDA"

My brother, Critter, and his wife, Stephanie, have a suite at the New Orleans Superdome for the Coldplay concert. They invited me to join them with my other family members and friends. It sounded surreal when my brother asked me, " Katie, do you want to bring a date?" I have been separated for almost a year, and my divorce is being finalized this week. It was the reality of my new reality. I have to say, I felt excited, nervous and very scared. My immediate response was, "Oh, my God! A date? No, thank you!" He asked, "Why not?" I responded, "I just don't want to. Regardless, I don't even know who I would ask."

Later on in the day, while I was walking back home from running on the track, I thought about my brother's question and I began to smile. I started laughing at the thought as I playfully asked Jesus, "Will You be my date?" I had a vision, He responded with excitement and a look of surprise, "I would love too!" He was smiling and laughing with a cute, little smirk on His face. He turned to me and jokingly asked, "What shall I wear?" I smiled back at Him, and I said in a fun way, "Ohhhhhhh, let's seeeeee…what about a pair of worn-in jeans, a faded vintage t-shirt with eagle wings spanning across the back and an old pair of rugged boots that look like they tell stories about all of your travels. Oh, and your hair down and slightly pushed back!" We both continued laughing and smiling at the thought. I turned to Jesus and in my own little, witty way, I said, "You see…You help me, and I help You! This is what partners are meant to do!" and the laughter continued.

Viva la Vida with Sweet Jesus!

3/28/09

Prayer: Sweet Jesus, I don't want the knowledge of what true
            love is. I want the experience. Please show me love.

I was praying, "Jesus, I don't want the knowledge of what true
love is. I want the experience! Please show me love!" He answered
my prayer in His own way. Through His Spirit, Jesus gave me the
experience of true love. With our solid foundation of mutual love,
respect and friendship—I now have the tools to recognize,
appreciate and nurture true love when it comes my way.

4/3/09

DO NOT BE AFRAID.

Yesterday, I pulled into a parking space at the grocery store when I heard the voice of Bette Midler singing the song, "The Rose." I never really listened to the words before, but something within me spoke, I heard, "Pay attention." I sat in my car, and as I listened to the song, my body temperature began to feel warmer, and a rush of emotions came out in tears. I quickly recognized that I was "The Rose."

"Some say love, it is a river that drowns the tender reed, some say love it is a razor that leaves your soul to bleed, some say love it is a hunger, an endless aching need, I say love it is a flower and you it's only seed. It's the heart afraid of breaking that never learns to dance, it's the dream afraid of waking that never takes the chance…"

When the song ends I hear Jesus speak to my heart, "Do not be afraid."

4/4/09

ACTION!

I woke myself up last night because I was repeating directions that were being given to me with heavenly authority, "I am to put my training and knowledge into action." I intuitively understood and acknowledged what I was being told, and I peacefully fell back asleep. I woke for a second time. I was speaking to Jesus, "Thank You so much for all of the beautiful treasures You have given to me. The peace, love and joy that I feel inside are so amazing." I realized what I was saying, knowing to whom I was speaking, and I fell back asleep with a great fullness in my heart.

When I woke up this morning and recalled the directions, I got excited! I am so grateful to know that we are making progress and staying in motion. Today, I will let the word, "ACTION" sink into my heart and run through my soul as I keep my eyes focused on Jesus and His way.

4/8/09

Prayer: God, please teach me to trust Your purpose.

I am back in Houston to meet with clients and have the divorce papers signed by the judge tomorrow. I am staying at The Houstonian. As I was meditating and praying this morning in my room, I heard Jesus speak to me. He said, "Today will be the day. Please remove all resistance." I understood it to mean that I would meet someone. I innocently and intuitively responded, "Teach me to trust Your purpose." He responded, "Live God's will." I sat in silence as curiosity began to rise.

It is so interesting to see how God places certain people in our lives for a purpose. I believe we often miss His intention. He can only guide so much, the rest is up to each of us to open our eyes and our heart and to take the time to discover that purpose. It may only take a moment to realize His intent or it may take years. Often, if we're not paying attention, we let amazing opportunities pass us by.

My prayer today is that we all slow down, open our eyes, open our hearts and listen to those around us. I pray we not only give a friendly smile and say, "It was nice to meet you," but rise to the challenge of taking it one step further. The challenge of not saying, "We should get together sometime," but rather, "When can we get together?" The "When can we get together?" is a step outside of my timid and non-aggressive personality. It is also something I feel God calling me to do.

I crawled into my comfy bed at The Houstonian this evening, and in my heart, I started talking to God, "God, I am really disappointed. I heard Jesus say this morning that I would be meeting someone. Well, the day has ended, and I did not meet anyone. I want You to know that I am not disappointed about not meeting someone, but I am disappointed in that maybe I am not hearing You clearly? What if all of these "messages" I receive are not from You, but rather just a figment of my imagination? What if my mind is just making all of this up? I am beginning to doubt myself again. Please talk to me. Let me know that it is You. Can this really be? Could I be wrong?" I lay silently in bed and my mind is still. I feel peace. My heart speaks, "I am accurate in that when I 'hear' Jesus I typically receive some sort of confirmation that what I've heard is valid. I have a good track record. There is just no way I can make this up, nor would I want to. I know I am creative, but I am not that creative. I also can't deny what huge strides have been made in bringing peace and order into my mind, body and soul. Not to mention, I can feel the Holy Spirit. I just can't make that up!" After this reasoning, I simply find peace in believing in God's word. I soon fall asleep.

4/10/09

Lesson: Take ACTION on God's direction.

Clue: "Whispering words of wisdom, let it be, let it be."

Yesterday was a huge day for me! As usual, I woke up in meditation and prayer. I heard Jesus speak the same message to me, "Today will be the day. Remove all resistance. Live God's will." I sighed deeply and was somewhat agitated. I slowly responded with fatigue, "God, I heard this message yesterday and nothing happened, but, I will pay attention, and I trust what You say." I suddenly received a very strong and loving feeling that rushed through my soul, and, once again, it overruled any doubt that lingered. I knew I needed to pay close attention.

     The court ruling went as expected, and I was relieved my divorce was finally official. I was confused in that I felt happiness in closing one door, but saddened that a decade of my life had ended just like that. Regardless, I took a deep breath, I walked out of the courthouse—exhaling what was and now, breathing in what is fresh, clean and sunny air. As I pulled out of the downtown parking lot I wondered where I should go. I had time to spare before I met with my client. I recalled Jesus telling me I was going to meet someone today. Thinking I was being clever, I decided to go to a hot Starbuck's location on West Gray in River Oaks. I parked my car, grabbed my paperwork and walked into Starbuck's with a new and nervous confidence. I was single, and I was free and as I stood in line, waiting to order my coffee, I thought, "Could this really be?" Suddenly, the gentleman behind me politely said, "You are a very beautiful woman." I smiled graciously, thanked him, and turned back around. I thought to myself, "Ah, this single woman needed to hear something positive!" He continued, "Not only are you beautiful, but I love the way you dress. You look very classy. That is nice to see." I thanked him again, and I told him I appreciated his kind words. I was now feeling really good. I was wearing a classic pin-striped, button down shirt with a solid white collar, form fitting blue jeans, a casual belt and low, sling-back stiletto's. I actually exclaimed within my heart, "Thank you, God! You knew I needed some encouragement today." I placed my order, picked up my coffee and went outside to find a table. I had a smirk on my face as I seriously thought, "I can't believe I am actually sitting here, hanging out at a Starbucks, thinking Prince Charming is going to approach me." Although, I found myself feeling completely ridiculous, I could not disregard the strong feeling I received during meditation that said I would be meeting someone today. I was simply trying to follow directions and allow myself to be open and available to someone or something that I was not really sure about. The clock continued ticking, and no one approached my table. I looked at my watch and realized it was time for my first meeting. I thought, "Oh well, it was worth a try, and at least I made an effort. Who knows what today will bring? I still feel good, and it is a beautiful day."

The day rolled on. There was not a cloud in the sky. All of my meetings went well, and the day was finally winding down. I had been invited to go to the River Oaks Tennis tournament that night by a dear friend of mine. By this time I wasn't in the mood to go to a party, and I was thinking a quiet dinner would be nice with another friend of mine. I picked up the phone to call Katherine and tell her I would not be joining her at the tennis tournament. Well, not to my surprise her response was, "I am not taking 'no' for an answer! Get over here! It is time for you to start living and having fun. I will meet you in the parking lot." I surrendered and cancelled my alternate dinner plans. As I parked my car in the parking lot, I got a very nervous feeling in my stomach. I was now officially divorced and single. I also knew I would be seeing people I had not seen in over a year. My earlier, newfound confidence was dwindling fast. I suddenly felt insecure and embarrassed that I was divorced. I tried to shake it off, and I walked nervously through the crowd and headed straight to a table in the back. It would serve as my hideaway. I thought if I just stayed right there not too many people would see me. Katherine introduced me to several of her friends I had never met, and we all sat around the table and talked. Knowing I had *just* been divorced, they all discussed potential dates for me. I felt dread in having to hit the dating scene. Hours went by and another dear friend of mine, Lisa, turned to me and said, "You've been sitting here all night. It's time for you to get up and start mingling." I looked at her like a wounded and lost puppy and whined with total dread, "I really don't want to. I feel uncomfortable." She looked at me and said, "You need to. Come on! " I hesitantly agreed and slowly rose from my chair. I had not even walked ten feet forward when I saw an old neighbor heading towards me, "Hey! I heard you're divorced! I have the most perfect person I want to set you up with." She was beginning to tell me about her divorced friend when I felt this tall presence moving towards me. I sensed someone standing near, and I heard a strong voice through the crowd, "Katie Ridgeway, Stanton Scott!" I turned my head, and I was completely surprised. Stanton and I both went to Ole Miss, and I had not seen him in over twenty years. We did not know each other well, but we both knew of each other. He smiled and quickly said, "I ran into Katherine. She said you just got divorced and that I should come find you." We were getting reacquainted when he looked at me, took a few steps back and exclaimed, "You look so good! You look great without that bleached blonde hair and heavy makeup!" I then took a step back in total disbelief at what he had just said. My first thought was, "I can't believe he just said that. What a jerk!" but as quickly as I had that thought, I could not help but to smile and laugh in agreement. It was so true! "Is that supposed to be a compliment?" I asked. He said in all sincerity, "Yes! You look so natural, and you are beautiful!" I smiled back, still laughing "Well then, I'll take it." Stanton and I stood there for some time catching up, laughing at old stories. Stanton then enthusiastically said, "I am here to show you a good time!" I was attracted to his positive energy, and his ability to make me laugh so easily. My tension soon faded, and I felt like me again! He suggested, "Why don't we go sit down at a table?" I tried to play it coy and tell him that I really needed to go find my friends, but he refused to listen. "Come on, Katie! You're in good hands with me!" He was so much fun, very persuasive and determined! I realized that his 6'4" frame was as large as his personality, and I soon gave into his request. He pointed out that we should sit down at the table near the swimming pool. A friend of Stanton's was getting up from the table just as we were approaching—he introduced us and before she left, she looked at me and gave me a thumb's up. I smiled, feeling that was a pretty good sign to take into consideration. The band across the pool had been on a break, but as soon as we sat down they returned and got into position. The first song they played was, "Let it Be" by the Beatles! Not only was the band playing the song, but Stanton, now facing me, started to loudly sing the words to me, "...whispering words of wisdom, let it be, let it be..." He paused, looked me directly in the eyes and asked in a serious tone, "Do you know who sings this song?" My jaw had already hit the table, and I was in complete and total disbelief at what was happening. I answered him with excitement and a new perspective, "Yes! The Beatles!" With a smile on his face, he said, "I like you already!" I looked up towards the sky and exclaimed from within myself, "OHHHHH, MY GOD! YOU JUST SET ME UP!" I was beaming with joy and smiling from ear to ear, realizing that I was clearly hearing God's directions. He was indeed helping me, and answering my prayers in His own way. At this point, I was too afraid to jump to any big conclusions, but what I did know for certain was that God was involved, and I needed to pay attention to what He wanted to show me. By choice, I decided to trust God and follow His lead.

The evening ran away as we were wrapped up in non-stop conversation, and before we knew it, the party was almost over. Stanton asked me if I would like to go out to dinner. I certainly was not ready for the night to end, so I happily agreed. As we stood up from the table, he turned towards me and he asked, "Is it alright if I hold your hand?" I hesitated. My first thought was, "No. I don't want anyone to see me leaving the party, holding someone's hand after I just got divorced this morning." But my feeling was, "I would love for you to hold my hand!" My response was, "Yes." He gently picked up my hand, looked at me smiling and said, "It's not so bad, is it?" I laughed, and I felt excited that someone was taking the lead. He felt strong, and I felt comfortable.

It was late, and Fleming's restaurant was about to close, but Stanton, knowing the hostess and staff all too well, talked them into serving us. His usual table was already taken so we sat at a new table, and we talked all night. I think deep down inside I wanted to test him. I knew that whomever I dated would need to be open to the depth of my spirituality. I know the reality and discomfort that the subject of religion often brings to people, and I also knew that I did not want to be with anyone who was not understanding and accepting of who I am—so I began to tell him about my intimate relationship with Jesus. He listened as I told him about some of my experiences, and he questioned the authenticity of what I was sharing with him. It was a challenge for me to defend my belief and answer the questions he presented. I remained steadfast in my faith, and I did not judge him for disagreeing with some of my beliefs. I respected and embraced his difference in opinion—I found it interesting. During our debate, Stanton suddenly placed his hand on mine, and he looked me straight in the eyes. He sincerely asked, "May I kiss you?" I looked at him intently, thinking about what my response was going to be. I sat in silence until I slowly began to smile at the thought. I wanted to kiss him, so once again, I answered, "Yes." He slowly leaned in towards me, and he gave me the softest and sweetest kiss imaginable. It was absolutely perfect! He casually sat back in his chair, and his eyes never left mine. Carefully, he began to speak, "I want you to know something. We have talked about some heavy subject matters tonight, and although some of your stories sound a little hokey to me, I want you to know one thing: most guys, after hearing your stories about running and interacting with Jesus would hit the door running. But I want you to look at where I am—I am sitting right here, by your side. I see that your faith has brought you peace and happiness, and that's what's important. I love that about you! That's the kind of guy I am." With those words spoken, I sat in silence staring deep into his eyes that seemed strangely familiar. My heart wanted to believe what he was telling me, and I knew that only time would tell me the truth. I was certain of one thing and that was: Let it be!

4/10/09

Lesson: Capitalize on every opportunity!

I woke up feeling overwhelmed with beautiful emotions, questions, confusion, and just complete awe as to what had transpired yesterday. I began thanking God. Although I felt scared, I promised God that I would open myself up to what He wants to show me. I simply could not deny the significance of meeting Stanton, the lessons and events that led up to our meeting, and the feelings he ignited within me. I was pouring over the details of the night while I was getting dressed and packing my suitcase to drive back to New Orleans when my phone began to ring. It was Stanton. He wanted to tell me he had a great time with me, and he asked if I would like to meet him for lunch before I left town. I joyfully accepted his invitation!

I approached Escalante's in Highland Village and began looking for a parking place—I quickly noticed Stanton sitting outside on the patio waiting for me, he smiled and waved as he saw me drive past him. I felt nervous butterflies and said out loud, "Ohhhhhh, God." I took a deep breath and tried to gather my emotions. I parked my car and made my way towards his table. He had a huge smile on his face, and I could see and feel his excitement at seeing me. I smiled back, laughing in thought, because I was feeling the same way that I knew he was feeling. He greeted me with a sweet, big hug and kiss. To no surprise, we had great conversation, and the lunch was full of laughter, and it just felt comfortable. I was cherishing every minute of whatever this was to be, and I was simply enjoying myself.

After time had passed, I told Stanton that as much as I wanted to stay, I had to get on the road. He walked me to my car. After saying our dreaded goodbye, he stood there looking into my eyes with a smile on his face. I returned the unspoken feeling with my eyes. He slowly leaned into me, and we kissed sweetly in perfect harmony. My stomach was doing somersaults, and I felt like I was floating! He was so gentle, yet I could feel his strength and passion. The moment and feeling was intense and neither one of us wanted it to end. We embraced each other more tightly in silence. I thought to myself, "This feeling is not normal. What's going on? Is this for real? This is crazy!" We literally could not let go of each other. Every time I would try to leave, I found myself back in Stanton's embrace. We simply could not part, so we decided to sit in my car to extend our time together. We talked, kissed, rested our foreheads together, and nuzzled our faces together as if we had known each other for years. Stanton quietly said, "This feels so nice, doesn't it?" I nodded my head in agreement. My head and my heart were spinning. We finally said goodbye, and I drove away thinking and feeling, "Oh, my God." I wanted to cry out—in excitement and out of fear.

4/11/09

Prayer: Sweet Jesus, I pray that this day brings new life to those who are suffering and joy to those who have been healed.

It is Easter! What a beautiful day to celebrate. This is an awesome reminder of the level of trust Jesus had in His Father. No amount of fear could deter His obedience to God's commands. I often think about Jesus praying in the garden the night before his crucifixion. I know how strong and courageous He is, but He is a human being. Don't we all have fears and doubts? I think about what He must have been thinking, feeling and what His actions are. I imagine him crying, trembling with a fear that He had never known before. His mind is tormented with emotional pain, and the reality of the physical pain He knows He will have to endure. He questions God as to why His command must be. He wonders why His only son must be crucified. He tells Him that He is frightened and scared. I imagine Him fearing the unknown—knowing enough to realize it would be extremely difficult and challenging. After time passes, Jesus understands with full certainty, whether He likes it or not, He must obey God's will. He must come to terms with His brutal death and simply, trust. He calms His fears by asking God to infuse Him with His strength and courage. I imagine Him becoming more at ease. He has conceded with his fate, and He is now at peace with what is about to happen. He understands tomorrow will bring great pain, but that it will pass—He will bring peace to the world. He is ready.

I pray this day brings new life to those who are suffering and joy to those who have been healed. I thank God for having the courage to sacrifice His only Son. I thank Jesus for being so brave. I respect Mary for demonstrating grace and faith through her Son's torment. I pray that we all optimize on the gifts that derived from Jesus's crucifixion.

4/15/09

Lesson: Healthy relationships come into existence when both partners are complete within themselves. You simply come together to share love, both giving and receiving.

Now that I am divorced, I have noticed more people confiding in me about their unhappy marriages. I have given this much thought, and I am convinced that healthy relationships only come into existence when both partners are complete within themselves. This relieves your partner of having to "feed" you and of you having to "feed" them. You simply come together to share an already fulfilled life. You simply want to love, to both give and receive, the ultimate gift in life.

I know that once I was filled with the Holy Spirit, my attitude and perspective on life and people changed dramatically for the better. The more joy you have in your soul, the more joy there is to share with others. It's when you're unhappy with yourself that you look to other people, things or activities to fill the void and make you feel better. When these people, things or activities fail to meet our eternal needs (which they eventually will), you blame others for what is really your own unhappiness. You find faults in everything and everyone around you—failing to look within yourself, the real source. If you can eliminate this void by filling your heart with God's love, you can stop looking for "happy substitutes." To know God intimately is to be completely fulfilled.

I am so thrilled at the thought of sharing my love and my peace with someone else. I pray that someone else wants to share love and peace with me. I meditate, and my heart quickly goes to, "Let it be!"

4/17/10

US, TOGETHER, IS ALL YOU WILL EVER NEED. THE TRUE
DESIRES OF YOUR HEART IS WHAT I WILL SHOW YOU,
BUT REMEMBER DESIRES AND NEEDS ARE TWO
DIFFERENT THINGS. DESIRES ARE TEMPORARY, NEEDS
ARE ETERNAL.

Jesus, although Stanton has come to me in the most amazing way,
I am still afraid at times. Please show me what You want me to
see. I no longer trust myself, but I do trust in You. I hear Jesus
speak softly, "Us, together, is all you will ever need. The true
desires in your heart are what I will show you. But remember,
desires and needs are two different things. Desires are temporary.
Needs are eternal."

I sit and reflect on what He just said. Words begin to flow to
me and I hear His Spirit, "Open your eyes, open your heart, follow
Me and I will take you to the start. This time will be different,
watch and you will see what beauty arrives when you allow Me, a
Gentleman, to lead. The days will be bright. The night is clear.
Truth be told, I AM HERE to watch you smile, to dry your tears.
You and I, TOGETHER WE APPEAR. We watch them wonder,
scratching their heads, LOVE is the answer, no words to be said.
The feeling is mutual, no denying the truth, what lies ahead is us:
SIMPLICITY IN LOVE AND TRUTH!

4/19/09

Lesson: The REAL YOU is always inside.

I went to my twenty-year high school reunion this past weekend. It was so much fun seeing people I had lost touch with. The most interesting fact was that no one had really changed. Hopefully, you grow, mature and develop your inner core, but I do believe our foundation is formed early in life, and although we may falter from our path, the real you is always inside.

At the reunion, one of my dear friends from grade school, Sheila, reminded me of a beautiful experience I had completely forgotten about. Once, in high school, Sheila and I were in Florida with my best friend, Nicole. We were all sitting outside on the deck of the rental house. It was a beautiful night. As we were talking, I looked up at the clear sky and saw a shooting star. Following the star, I saw a large, bright angel appear and quickly rescind. I was so taken back and in shock at what I had seen that I became full of emotion, silent and barely able to speak. My friends, confused at what just came over me, questioned me. I told them what I had just seen. I told them that I knew it sounded crazy, but I was certain it was a large, glowing angel.

I know, in my heart, that the Holy Spirit reminded my friend of that story so she would share it with me. It was a special memory. It is a reminder to me that heavenly hosts have always been present and so has my spirituality.

The next day, Sheila told her mom that she saw me at the reunion. She told her all about my growing spirituality. Her mom, also strong in faith, reminded Sheila, "Do you remember how Katie saw that angel in the sky when you all were in Florida?" For me, that was confirmation that I was to be reminded of that experience. What are the chances of her mother reminding Sheila about that one story in particular? A story I had forgotten about!

On a lighter and funnier note, Sheila reminded me of a few other stories. She reminded me I had a crush on one of the handsome, young priests at school. I cringed when I had to confess my sins to him. I remember feeling so embarrassed to tell him all of my inner failings, but I did it anyway. Secondly, she reminded me of a time when we were in religion class at Ursuline Academy, and I showed her a picture of Jesus saying, "How fine is Jesus?" After that statement, she burst into shock and laughter, "Katie! That is Jesus you are talking about! I swear, only you would say that!" I responded very innocently and sincerely, "But, He is."

Like I said, we may get off course, we may move to different cities, we may meet new people and yet, WE ARE WHO WE ARE! Some things simply do not change.

4/22/09

Challenge: "Do you believe in what you feel?"

Stanton and I have been talking on the phone non-stop—we have amazing conversations for hours on end. I was scheduled for a Houston trip, to meet with my clients, and I happily added dinner with Stanton on my to-do list. I was staying at The Houstonian, and on the night of our date I told Stanton that I would be waiting downstairs. I walked in the bar, ordered a glass of wine and sat down at a table close to the window so I could watch for him. I slowly sipped my drink, gazing out the window in great anticipation of seeing Stanton again. I saw a silver convertible sports car whiz into the front entrance. The valet rushed over to the driver's side, and out stepped a tall, young man. There he was, right on time! He looked even more handsome than I remembered, and I felt truly excited. I watched him take long strides across the drive and quickly up the walkway. I was trying to look relaxed and calm when he walked in to greet me. He saw me from across the room and immediately, his face lit up with a huge, warm smile. As he approached me, he opened his arms up as wide as he could, and he loudly exclaimed, "Katie! It is sooooo good to see you! I missed you!" He hugged me so big and tight that he literally lifted my feet up off of the ground. It felt awesome, and it was so refreshing to have someone *verbalize* their feelings and *show* their excitement and genuine happiness. Most men totally hide their feelings, trying to play it cool. My initial thought was, *Wow! I really like what I am seeing. I love his enthusiasm!*

We sat down and talked for a few minutes, eventually heading off to his parked car. As we were walking, I could feel the immense energy and excitement flowing through both of us. We could not stop smiling and looking at each other, trying to take it all in. At the same time, this unusual level of comfort was present. As we drove to the restaurant, The Grove, the song, "In the Waiting Line" by Zero 7 began to play in his car. The tune immediately caught my attention, and I started listening to the words carefully as the lead sang, "Waiting line, till' your time, ticking clock, everyone stop, everyone's saying different things to me, different things to me…do you believe in what you feel?" I sat in my seat, and I could feel it. Something much bigger than myself, an electric energy filled the car. I took a deep breath in, and silently said to myself, "Jesus, what is this?" And the line from the song played in my heart again, "Do you believe in what you feel?" I knew.

We happily walked in The Grove together, holding hands so naturally as if we had been together for years. There was a wait for our table, so we went to the bar, sat down and ordered a drink. We simply could not take each other in enough. It just felt right! Eventually, the hostess seated us at our table and we squeezed in a cozy booth, sitting very closely to one another. We couldn't help but to continue to stare at each other and simply smile. The waitress approached our table and asked how she could help us. Stanton playfully said, "We are celebrating our anniversary today!" I began to laugh, as did he, and the waitress congratulated us. He just continued to smile as he looked at me, and I went along with it as he placed our order. I knew at that point that I loved what I was seeing and feeling. He was just fun! We both giggled and stared at each other, holding on to every word that each spoke. I realized we were both acting like teenagers on a date. It felt like we had been together forever, and when I would look into his eyes, it was as if I could see right through him—they seemed so familiar to me. I couldn't figure it out. It was the most amazing emotion to experience. I remember Stanton leaning back from me at one point, wanting to get me in his full view, and he started shaking his head from side to side as he smiled. Even though I knew what he was feeling, because our chemistry was explosive on all levels, I coyly asked, "What?" and he responded, "You are trouble!" I knew exactly what he meant, because I also knew that he was trouble. Good trouble.

As the dinner came to an end, the waitress presented us with a dessert plate—she placed the piece of cake in front of us, and written along the side of the plate, it read, "Happy Anniversary." We smiled, laughed and thanked her for the dessert. We looked at each other, kissed sweetly and said, "Ohhhh, our anniversary! Our first 'official' date." I knew in my heart, it was the first anniversary with many more to follow.

As I was driving back to New Orleans the next day, I felt such excitement and joy thinking about my date with Stanton. I also had a sudden feeling of fear. I was afraid of the overwhelmingly beautiful feelings that I felt. Fear began to wash over me in a violent rush. My head was not allowing my heart to relish in happiness. My mind began to flood with thoughts such as, "This is too soon. You will get hurt. Don't be so vulnerable. How do you know he is not feeding you a bunch of lies? He's playing you, and you are falling for it!" I realized my joy had completely vanished, and it was replaced with fear and anxiety. I turned off my radio. I began to pray hard with all that is in me, with full heart, feelings and emotion. I am practically in tears crying out, "Jesus, please, please, You need to help me. I am so scared. I am feeling feelings I have never felt before. I feel like it is way too soon to feel this way. I don't trust what I am feeling because I am so scared. I do not want to get hurt again. Can you please reassure me that Stanton has been sent by You? Anything, just some sort of sign. I know I am to trust You, and I do, but I don't trust myself. I know You do not have to prove Yourself to me or to anyone, that I am to simply trust, but this is not about Your abilities—this is about mine! What if I am getting this wrong? I am begging You for discernment! I am begging You for Your wisdom! Please somehow show me this opportunity is from You, and that I am not being deceived. I need You!" I remind myself to relax. I immediately hear a text message hit my iPhone. I pick it up, and it's from Stanton! He tells me what a wonderful time he had last night, and that he is simply thinking about me. He said that he is already anticipating my next trip back to Houston. I began to smile, again, thinking about how nice it is for him to tell me that he is thinking about me. I think about how most men would hide their thoughts, play it cool, fearing that if they seem too interested, too soon, they will look desperate or be too vulnerable. I begin to feel relief, and just as I did, I turn my head to the left, and I see a large billboard on I-10 as I'm approaching Beaumont, Texas. The billboard is the image of Divine Mercy, the very image of Jesus that I meditate on every morning! There He was with His perfect timing, revealing Himself to me again, with one arm raised and His other hand resting on His heart as the rays of blood and water come forth—on the billboard, below the image of Jesus, it reads, "Jesus, I trust in You." I burst out into tears, and I thank Him for helping me, for showing me that He is *really* with me, guiding me and protecting me—always.

4/23/09

Prayer: Sweet Jesus, show me the love!

As I continue to exclaim, "Jesus, show me what I'm looking for!" I see myself in one of the movie scenes from *Jerry McQuire*, but instead of shouting with all enthusiasm and gusto, "Show me the money!" I am saying, "Show me the love!" I made a promise to Jesus to surrender my desires to God. I joyfully invited Him into my life so He could show me what I was looking for, not for me to show Him what I think I want. I feel extremely confident in God! I know He will place me on the right path. I feel scared and vulnerable, but at the same time I am so excited. This is going to be fun!

4/26/09

TAKE A STEP BACK. GIVE ME THE ROOM I NEED. UNDERSTAND THAT YOU WILL NOT ALWAYS UNDERSTAND.

Lord, as much fun as I just said this was going to be, and although you have shown me Your hand in meeting Stanton, I am still scared. I hate when I doubt and contradict everything I know to be true.

I sit in mass, and I am not paying attention to the homily. My thoughts are racing with my own fears and questions, and I stare straight ahead at Jesus on the crucifix. I pray my own prayers silently, "Jesus, I know You know the confusion I feel right now in this very moment. I ask for You to please guide my thoughts and grant me the wisdom, understanding and discernment I need. I do trust in You, but I am having trouble trusting myself and trusting what I hear You say to me. What if I am not understanding You clearly?" I pause and I reflect in silence. I hear Jesus speak to me, "Take a step back. Give Me the room I need. Let it be. Do not be afraid. Everything I have revealed to you has come to fruition. How many more times must I show you? Do not doubt you are hearing Me when I speak to you." My eyes fill with tears and an expansive wave of warmth fills my chest. I feel full, and I feel protected. This feeling gives me the knowledge the Holy Spirit is with me right now. As I relish in this beautiful emotion, I can't help but to feel disappointment in myself. Disappointed that I doubt myself so often. I wonder why it's so difficult for me to believe what I know to be true. I reflect on what Jesus speaks to me so often, "Understand that you will not always understand." I repeat this over and over in my head so it will sink in and replace all of my doubts with sheer confidence.

I understood—I was beginning to encroach on God's path for me. I must take a step back, and allow Him to work. I must understand that although it is not my plan, it is HIS PLAN. Someone very wise continuously tells me, "Katie, Carpe diem! Carpe diem! Live in the moment, and let it be!" My friend is Stanton.

4/27/09

DO NOT RESIST WHAT IS. SURRENDER. ALLOW YOUR HEART TO FEEL AGAIN.

As I start my new single life, I realize how difficult it is for me to let go of all the pain I have held on to for so long. I try to be strong, and I try to put myself back out in the world, but then I freeze. I try to relax, yet I tense up. I am so afraid of being hurt in a relationship. It is frightening to allow your heart to be vulnerable. I reflect on what I have learned from my past. I feel confident in what I should look for, and how I should feel. I know that Jesus is with me, guiding me. But, why am I still fearful? It is a great challenge to let go of how I THINK my life should unfold and to truly surrender my thoughts and my ways into the Hands of God. It sounds so assuring and comforting, but I find it to be absolutely frightening! I am losing control, literally. I must allow God to put people and opportunities in my path, and it is my job and *my responsibility* to be open to new ideas, new thoughts and new feelings, and explore what He is trying to show me. Think about it, allowing someone else to control all areas of your life, including your love life! I know that in order for this to work, I must invite God into my life daily, and share every thought with Him—it must be personal, intimate and communicative—just as any healthy relationship should be. We must *both* give and receive. In the past, I was embarrassed to share my deepest thoughts and desires with Jesus, realizing that they are not always pure (as if He didn't know what I was really thinking anyway). Finally, I got over it, and I came clean with all of my thoughts and actions. I actually felt such great relief and freedom in knowing that there was absolutely nothing left to hide. He knows every intimate detail about me, and I can tell Him anything without feeling guilty, ashamed or judged.

I suddenly saw myself as an open book, smiling in confidence, knowing who I am as I stand tall, in front of Jesus, and I proudly announce, "Here I am! This is me! All of me!" I see Jesus, so casual in His manner and demeanor, looking at me and saying, "Finally!" We laugh and hug each other tightly in excitement over forming our new, *open* and everlasting bond of friendship.

I know that by inviting, and I choose that word carefully, *inviting* Jesus into *all* areas of my life—He now has *my permission* to help me. Once again, I look Jesus in the eyes, "Please, show me what I'm looking for." He responds, "Do not resist what is. Surrender. Allow your heart to feel again."

4/29/09

TRUST ME! TRUST ME! TRUST ME!

I realize it is much easier to say what you want to do than to actually live it out and do it. I thought I had overcome my self-doubt. Apparently, I still need work. I thought about Jesus's words to me, "Action. It is time to put your knowledge and words into practice." I knew exactly what He meant. I have the knowledge and the tools, but I must learn how to apply them into making choices in life, and be confident in doing so. As I squat down to stretch my legs as I prepare for a run, Jesus looks into my eyes and speaks, "Trust Me. Trust Me. Trust Me." We slowly stand back up, and He reminds me to never lose sight of Him, and I nod in agreement. I turn on my iPod, and we take off running to Eddie Money playing in my ear. I smiled listening to the words, "Baby, hold on to me. Whatever will be, will be. The future is ours to see, so, baby, hold on to me...don't be thinkin' about what's not enough now. Just be thinkin' about what you got...think of all my lovin now, I'm gonna give you all I got...momma's always told me that money can't buy you love..." I thought to myself, laughing, "How perfect!"

5/1/09

Lesson: Happiness comes from within. It does not come from someone or something.

Trust. Trust is something I could not grasp, not only with God, but also in my personal relationships. Why couldn't I apply it? After contemplation, I realize it is hard for me to trust people because I have no control over their thoughts or actions. I want to overcome this issue. I ask Jesus, "How do I establish trust in a relationship? I know this needs to be the foundation, but how do I pour the foundation?"

I pause, listen, and I write what I hear. "It starts from the very beginning. The moment that truth begins to reveal itself is in the small ways that most people would feel are insignificant. Does this person speak their mind? Does this person make direct eye contact? Does this person walk in confidence, or do they walk in shame and fear? What kind of spirit does this person resonate? How do they treat others? How do they react when something does not go accordingly? What is their behavior and their reactions when they've had a bad day? How do they treat their family members? Friends? What are their values and beliefs? Most importantly, how do they treat themselves?"

As I continue to date Stanton, as frightened as I am, I made a promise to J.C. this morning—I will surrender it all to Him. My goal is not to just live in the moment, which I feel I have accomplished in my daily routines, but to also live in the moment as I begin to date! I will surrender myself to God and give Him the room to work. I will meet each individual with an open heart and with open eyes. Most importantly, I will use my best assessment and not the judgment of others. I will remind myself that I have the wisdom and knowledge to form my own opinions. I have to learn how to speak truth in all ways, hurtful or not. I deserve to be happy, and I will not forfeit my own happiness in an effort to try to make someone else happy—that is not my responsibility. Happiness comes from within, it does not come from someone or something. What I do believe and pray for today is to *share* happiness, truth, love and respect with a life partner.

5/4/09

STOP RUNNING IN A CIRCLE OF FEAR. TRUST ME
ENOUGH TO MOVE FORWARD, KNOWING THAT I WILL
CATCH YOU BEFORE YOU FALL.

My daughter, Sophia just turned six. She was determined to take
her training wheels off of her bike. She was very nervous, and she
expressed this to me over and over again, but she was still willing
and determined to try. We walked over to the Country Day football
field in an attempt to help pad a potential fall. I gave her some
pointers, and I reminded her to stay balanced, look straight ahead,
to stay in motion by pedaling continuously and to trust me enough
to know that I will catch her before she falls. I repeated, "Do not be
afraid!"

     She climbed up on her bike. She repeatedly turned her head
back to reassure herself I was still there, but when she did, she lost
balance and focus. I repeated, "I am here! I am here! I will not let
you fall! Stop turning around!" Sophia continued to yell, "I am
scared! I can't do this!" I continued to tell her otherwise. She was
also having difficulty holding the handle bars straight, so we were
literally going around in circles. Sophia was unable to get the
rhythm, balance and momentum she needed. We rested, and I gave
her a pep talk. She pouted, sadly saying, "I can't do it." I told her,
"You will not be able to do it if you don't believe you can do it.
Try again." Sophia slowly picked herself up and got back on her
bike. I began to push her from behind, and she started chanting,
"Pedal, pedal, pedal, pedal, pedal." I felt her finding her balance,
so I slowly let go of her bike—off she went, with me running
closely behind. I began to chant with her, "Pedal, pedal, pedal,
pedal," so she could hear me—I wanted her to hear my voice so
she would be assured I was right there with her. When she finally

came to a stop, she jumped off her bike and started shouting for joy. I exclaimed, "You did it! You did it!" We gave each other a high five, and in excitement she screamed, "That was awesome! That was so much fun! I want to do it again! As soon as I started saying, 'pedal,' I stopped thinking about what I was doing. It made me think about something else." I agreed with enthusiasm, and I told her, "Yes, you stopped focusing on your fear, and it came to you naturally!" As I said all of these things to Sophia, I realized this is exactly what Jesus has been trying to teach me as well! I had an opportunity to see and to feel Jesus's role in my life, obviously in a very simple way, but it made me realize how detrimental fear is to progress. It made me see how fear holds you back, keeps you from moving forward and how crucial it is to trust. I also recognized why I hear Jesus speak to my heart—He wants me to *hear His voice*, so I can be confident in knowing *He is with me in Spirit*. With that realization, I hear Jesus speak to me, "Just as you were there for Sophia, and just as you would not allow her to fall— how could you ever think I would allow you to fall? Stop running in a circle full of fear. Trust me enough to move forward, knowing that I am with you, and I will catch you before you ever fall. Trust! Enjoy your ride, and live in peace and freedom! Allow joy and happiness to touch *all* areas of your life and those around you. I will never leave you. Do not be afraid."

5/11/09

Meditate: What is your vision of love?

Father Joe, a family friend, asked me a question a few weeks ago. He asked me to think about *my definition of love*. I realize the significance of his question, especially as I open myself up to a new relationship. My first thought went to the Bible verse in the book of John, "Love is patient, love is kind, love is not jealous..." Yes, I do believe that is the definition of love, but what I have learned is that people express love in many different ways. I know I need to take it a step further. Suddenly, I hear, "What is your vision of love? What do you see you and your partner sharing? What are your actions, your communications, your feelings? Tell Me, what do you see?"

I reflect. I slowly respond—I see myself waking up in the morning, turning towards my partner and feeling so grateful to share my life with someone loving, kind, open and honest. I trust that what we share with each other is 100% authentic. I see us communicating about every aspect of our lives and our children's lives. I see us being genuinely excited to see each other at the end of every day. I see laughter. I see romantic dinners. I hear whispers of heartfelt feelings and emotions. I hear the inner voice speaking all thoughts and truth. I see an abundance of hugs and kisses. I feel safety in the arms of my partner, and I feel protection and great love. I feel someone who is gentle, yet strong, honest, compassionate, kind, loving, playful, wise and challenging. We travel and we explore. There is excitement and positive energy between us. I feel peace and love. We compliment each other— where one is strong the other is weak and vice versa, therefore, the balance is healthy. We grow, and we learn from each other. We respect each other. We love unconditionally, and we always work through our differences, as it is a compromise. We live our lives to the fullest, and we simply have no regrets.

5/17/09

Relish in Jesus in times of joy and be grateful that you have His
love and strength to draw on in times of pain and sorrow.

My daughter Susan is making her first communion today.
Yesterday, there was a retreat at the church for the parents and
children. As we all gathered around the room, Father Stephen
asked each of us, including the parents, for what we are most
grateful. As we went around the room, it was no surprise to me that
every parent responded with, "I am most grateful for my family." I
agree—family is truly a blessing, but my heart's first response was,
"I am most grateful for my relationship with Jesus." which is what
I said. I was not trying to be different. I was simply speaking the
truth.

    My thought today is simply a question, "Why don't we
choose Christ first?" My belief is that when we choose Christ first,
we are not choosing to love Jesus more than we love our family. It
is simple—it is only through God's love that we are taught how to
love others, *unconditionally*.

5/23/09

DO NOT CHOOSE TO NOT SEE WHAT NEEDS TO BE SEEN. WHAT NEEDS TO BE SEEN IS REALITY.

I meditate this morning and my pen begins to flow with the following words: "Do not set yourself up in wishful thinking and in false promises. This equates a false reality, which leads to disappointment. Do set yourself up in truth. Keep your eyes wide open. Do not choose to not see what needs to be seen. What needs to be seen is reality."

5/25/09

Lesson: The only way to truly learn is through experience, and
with experience will come both joy and pain.

Sweet Jesus, please remind me that I will not always make the
right choices in life and, I am only human. Remind me that
although I will make mistakes along the way, You will be graceful
enough to transform them to my advantage and to the advantage of
others. Remind me that the only way to learn is through
experience, and that with experience comes both joy and pain.
Remind me that in times of joy, You will sing along with me to
rejoice and in times of pain and sorrow, You will comfort me and
dry my tears. Remind me that life can only be lived one day at a
time. Remind me to live it to the fullest. Remind me that You are
with me every single step of the way. Remind me not to live in
fear, but rather to live in confidence through Spirit.

5/29/09

DO NOT GIVE UP. WHEN YOU WANT TO QUIT THAT MEANS GET UP AND GET GOING!

I was really struggling the other day. I felt opposition in almost every area of my life—personal, financial and family matters. I was so beaten and worn down. I soon had a vision of myself falling to the floor, wanting to give up, crying out in exhaustion. But, every time I had that pitiful thought, I could see Sweet Jesus standing over me, looking down at me and firmly saying, "Do not give up. When you want to quit, that means get up and get going!" I responded in a weary voice, "I am too tired," but as soon as I spoke those words, I suddenly remembered I had no choice but to keep moving forward. As I looked up at Jesus, I asked, "How?" He was looking into my tired eyes, and He said, "With Me." I continued to lay on the ground, still and unable to move. I wearily spoke, "I need to walk on Your feet. I simply can't move." Jesus reached His hand out to me so He could help me get up, and He said with a smile, "The pleasure is all mine." We continued to look at each other until our hands met for a sweet embrace. I slowly stood up, and just as a child would, I stepped up onto His feet, and I held onto Him as He began to walk for us. I felt so tired and absolutely foolish, but I knew I needed Him to carry me home. As I tried to keep my balance and remain planted on His feet, I looked up at Him, and I suddenly burst out into full laughter. There I was, a grown woman, walking on Jesus's feet! He began to smile and laugh with me. He spoke with such excitement, "I'll do whatever it takes! Just hold on to Me!" The laughter continued as we slowly walked our walk.

The next day I thought about the image of me walking on Jesus's feet. Without fail, I would break out into a huge smile and laugh, thinking about how silly it was I had this vision. I spoke to myself, "You really made that one up! It is so childish and ridiculous." I questioned, as I usually do, "Is this for real? I must be imagining this. It is too unbelievable!" I even took it as far as saying to myself, "Have you seen anyone doing that lately? What made you think about walking on feet?" and my response to myself was, "No, I have not seen anyone do that in years, but maybe it was just a random thought." I left it at that—although I absolutely loved my vision!

The very next day, I went to Susan and Sophia's review for their ballet recital. The teacher had warned us that it would be a long afternoon because all of the classes would have to run through their numbers. As I sat in the bleachers at the Country Day gym for over two hours, I began to feel restless. I stared out onto the gymnasium floor with my chin in my palm, and I saw a group of precious girls lining up for their dance. What I could not figure out was why a group of fathers stood off to the side, holding bouquets of flowers. I straightened up out of curiosity, trying to see what was going on. The music started playing and one father at a time began to walk center stage, meeting their daughters halfway. As they approached each other, the little girls slowly climbed up on their father's feet, and they began to dance! You can only imagine the disbelief at what I was seeing! I began to smile from ear to ear, and I began to laugh to myself, shaking my head, as I said, "Ohhhhhhh, my God! You are too funny! Thank You for revealing Yourself to me through the vision of my heart! It was Jesus!" I reminded myself that I am a child—just as these little girls are dependent on their father's lead—I am still dependent on my Father's lead. I am simply proud to call God, my Father. I am so thankful to be dancing on His feet!

6/4/09

Action: I can only thank God by living my life as it was
            designed to be.

Sweet Jesus,
You ignite my soul
Time and time again,
Only to reveal the beauty from within.
The love we share is bold and bright—
I simply can't describe the feelings I hold so tight.
You reveal the innocence in me
Love that we share so peacefully,
A partnership so grand only truths be told,
I can only thank You by living my life as it was designed to be
Honoring and respecting both You and me.

6/10/09

Believe: Look at the stars, look how they shine for you and
everything you do.

Last night was the Coldplay concert in New Orleans. It was
awesome! I could not help but to imagine the Spirit of Sweet Jesus
sharing in our laughter and enjoying the gift of amazing music—
smiling as He stands in His peaceful, cool, laid-back manner.

The highlight of the night was Chris Martin playing,
"Yellow." It is one of my favorite songs, and I can feel the words. I
also happen to love the color yellow for so many reasons—it is
happiness, it is bright and cheerful, and it has warmth that glows
and resonates in a room. It brings me back to memories of sunny
days and summer fun, relaxing poolside or sitting out in freshly cut
grass, sunglasses on, breathing in fresh air while just chilling. As I
listen to, "Yellow," I see us, me and Jesus. And as the words play,
I can hear Him sing to me, "Look at the stars. Look how they shine
for you and everything you do. Yeah, they were all yellow. I came
along. I wrote a song for you and all the things you do. And, it was
called, yellow...you know, you know I love you so much. You
know I love you so much...for you, I'd bleed myself dry, for you
I'd bleed myself dry..."

6/19/09

Lesson: Pay attention to details. Be open to all forms of communication.

I am back in Houston. Stanton and I went to go see a movie. As we were leaving the theatre, Stanton looked at me and asked, "Katie, what is seven times eight?" My heart fell to the floor, as did my jaw. I exclaimed in total shock and disbelief, "Fifty-six! What just made you ask me that?" He casually responded, "I have no idea? It just came out." I responded with excitement, "When I was young, I could never remember what seven times eight was until my grandfather, Gramps, whom has since passed away, taught me a little trick—he said, with a cute, little whistle, accentuating the sound of the "S" "Katie, sssseven times eight isssss fiffffffty-sssssssixxxx." I laughed so hard, repeating his trick, and from that day forward, I have never forgotten that seven times eight is fifty-six. It became our personal joke, and when we would see each other we would say, in our whistle, "Hey! sssssseven times eight issss fiffffffffty-sssssixxxxx!"

A huge lump formed in my throat, and I felt my heart expand. I knew, that once again, Gramps was teaching me a little trick—a simple form of communication, through others, to let me know that he is with me on this journey. I looked up at Stanton, "Gramps wanted to let me know that he is giving you his blessing."

I love the reality of life after death, and the existence of angels! I love you, Gramps, and, thank you for your blessing!

6/23/09

I WILL TAKE CARE OF YOU!

Sweet Jesus, just as You promised me, "I will take care of you!" Thank you for taking care of me. I see your beautiful design beginning to slowly unfold, one day at a time. I am learning—the more I trust in You, the better results I see. I remain calm and at peace as I wait for Your plan to come together.

On November 2, 2008, I found a book of my mother's called, *Novena, The Power of Prayer*, by Barbara Calamari and Sandra DiPasqua. I had never said a novena before, nor did I really understand what they were about (other than praying a prayer in repetition). I read the introduction to learn more. In summary, a novena is a prayer repeated to obtain a requested intention or spiritual grace. It can express one's willingness to accept divine intervention in the solution of a problem. The repetition of prayer helps to gradually clear the mind of all distractions in order to put focus on the requested intention. The novena should not be looked upon with superstition. It is used merely to develop a habit of addressing a higher power. With that said, I found a novena to St. Raphael in hopes of meeting a life partner. I said the novena, with conviction, from November 2, 2008 to November 11, 2008 and continued to say a personal prayer to St. Raphael from that day forward. I assumed it would take years to come to fruition, but in my heart I knew when the time was right, an opportunity to discover my life partner would present itself. I believe my opportunity is Stanton!

6/24/09

LOOK NOT SO MUCH AS TO WHAT PEOPLE SAY; WATCH WHAT THEY DO. CONSISTENCY IN BEHAVIOR AND PERFORMANCE OVER TIME, THIS WILL BE YOUR TRUTH.

Jesus, help me! I am scared. I feel love! I try to fight it off out of fear, but love is stronger and it continually comes back into my heart. Am I using good judgment? Am I overlooking things that need to be seen? Am I being naïve? I hear Jesus ask me, "Why do you focus on the negative? What do you feel that is positive?" I respond quickly, "I feel genuine love, and I feel genuinely loved. I feel like I have finally found someone who expresses their innermost thoughts (good and bad), someone who wants to share a life with me, someone who wants to build a family together, and someone who wants to protect me. Stanton can read my mind like no other (that is other than You). He tells me things that You share with me, unknowingly, of course—this morning he sent me a text message while I was in prayer—it said, "Good morning, Sunshine!" which is what you tell me, and I have never told a soul about that, nor has anyone else ever addressed me as that—there are no coincidences! When I look into his eyes, I get lost. I feel like I have known him before, or that we have known each other for a lifetime. I have feelings that I have never experienced before. I feel unusually comfortable with Stanton—I am happy just simply being with him. When he holds me, I can truly feel his love for me. We speak through songs. We think the same thoughts. He is kind and so very thoughtful. He makes me smile and laugh. He knows how to draw emotions out of me that, out of pain, I have buried. We love many of the same things, yet we are very different. In the end, we completely balance each other out, and I believe he is my soul mate.

Having said that, this relationship that I prayed for is exactly what scares me! Stanton is not the most popular choice among some people because he has a very strong personality, and he has no filter when he speaks. To some, this can come across as being very rude and crass—you either love him for who he is, or you are completely offended by him. You specifically told me, "Pray for a detachment from other people's opinions." I believe You taught me this lesson in order to prepare me for this very circumstance. You did also mention that it would pertain to someone that I would fall in love with, but I was to trust You. I swore that I would do what made me happy, not others. I still can't help but wonder, "Am I being fooled?" Jesus, my question to You is this, "When do you listen to opinions? Does it count for something? Or, not?" I listen, and I sit in silence until I hear, "In the past, have you listened to opinions of others regarding an individual's reputation? What was your *personal experience* with that person? Did your experience match the opinions of others?" I answer, "No, not always. I have often experienced something completely different." Jesus asked, "Did you not just answer your own question? Think about how unfortunate it is that so many relationships dissolve, or for that matter, never develop because of opinions—opinions that are not necessarily formed from experience. What counts is what your experience tells you. Remember this, and use it as your guide: Listen not so much as to what someone says. Watch what they do. Consistency in behavior and performance over time, this will be your truth."

6/29/09

Lesson: When you ask God for something, He does not just simply give it to you. What He does provide is the opportunity to earn your request.

Sweet Jesus, I remember reading that when you ask God for something, He does not just simply give it to you. That is too easy and there is no challenge or perseverance required, not enough learned. What He does give you is an opportunity. I need to remember this as I ask God to grant me so many gifts. When I ask God for courage, He does not simply give me courage, He gives me the opportunity to be courageous. When I ask God to remove fear, He does not simply remove it for me. He gives me the opportunity to face my fears. When I ask God to show me true love, He does not just give me true love. He gives me the opportunity to find and discover true love. In my heart, I know the opportunities that I have been praying for are right in front of me. Now, it is up to me to *take action*. I am ready!

7/10/09

Thanksgiving: Sweet Jesus, thank You for providing me with amazing opportunities!

Today, I will introduce someone very special to my family. Stanton is coming to New Orleans! Although I don't know what the future holds, I trust in Jesus. I trust that I am learning from every experience. I am facing my fears! Jesus, thank You for these amazing opportunities!

7/16/09

Lesson: God does not fail. The only failure that exists is in the one who does not listen, or in the one who listens, but fails to act.

Jesus, I am so impressed. I never thought that I would be able to *truly live in the moment*, but thanks to You, now, I know how. Your lessons, although very difficult, have been worth every second because through my pain, freedom was found. What an awesome relief!

Total dependence on God and God alone, still and always, my number one goal. I recognize that God does not fail. The only failure that exists is in the one who does not listen, or in the one who listens, but fails to act. My prayer today is that I not only listen to God, but that I act on God's word and fulfill my promise. Amen!

7/19/09

Lesson: There are NO COINCIDENCES!

Last week, Stanton and I went to church when he was in New Orleans. The homily resonated in my heart. The priest stated over and over again, very firmly, "THERE ARE NO COINCIDENCES!" Once again, it is confirmation to me! He also made a few points that struck me to the core.

> Jesus required His disciples to carry a walking stick for balance, which was needed at all, times. God is the walking stick.

> Jesus called out the disciples in pairs. Two disciples together at all times. This is a message that Jesus has sent to me on multiple occasions. I would hear, "Two is better than one."

> Wipe the dust off of your feet! The dust is fear, holding onto your past pain and hurts and not forgiving. Dust will slow you down and prevent progress.

Thank you for the reminders!

7/20/09

GET THE BALL ROLLING.

Last week, Jesus repeated, "Get the ball rolling." Obviously, He saw me dragging my feet on starting new projects. Jesus can prompt me all day long, but in the end, the outcome is my responsibility. I really don't know what I am doing, but I am just going to roll with the leads He sends me and explore what comes my way. I know that in time and with perseverance, what needs to be discovered will somehow reveal itself.

It is my belief that once you surrender to God, the power of the Holy Spirit prompts and guides our thoughts in order to direct us. It is willpower that turns the thought into action. Prayer unites the soul with God's will, creating an opening to receive, focusing on the positive and eliminating obstacles from your mind—believing in something greater than yourself. Move over ego!

7/24/09

Challenge: Fight fear! Learn trust. Fight doubt! Embrace truth.

While I was running the other day, all I could do was thank God over and over again. I am so grateful to have found freedom! As I reflect on all of the beauty in my life—I run smiling, and feel endless joy. I soon recognize a familiar runner headed in my direction. As she approaches me, I see she's practicing throwing punches just as a boxer would in a ring, as if she is training to fight. I see it as a reminder to continue fighting through my greatest obstacles, doubt and fear. Immediately, my heart has a vision: I am in a boxing studio and there is a large, red punching bag staring at me. On one side of the bag, in big, bold, white letters, the word "Doubt" runs vertically, on the other side it reads, "Fear." Jesus is training me. He asks me to throw strong punches and high leg kicks at the punching bag while instructing me to associate feelings to these actions to fight through negative emotions. The fighter in me comes out strong as I begin to work, "Fight fear! Learn trust. Fight Doubt! Embrace truth." As I repeat, "Fight fear!" I step away from the punching bag, turn to Jesus and embrace Him with love as I repeat, "Learn trust." I repeat the same action, fighting doubt and embracing truth. I must continue to practice, as practice soon becomes habit.

8/2/09

Meditate: Feel the energy that the Holy Spirit provides. Allow
the energy to carry you to your destination.

I know it sounds arrogant, but I feel something significant
transforming in my soul. I feel it stirring deep inside—it is
peaceful, calming, yet strong and exciting. I feel my destiny within
reach. Everyday, I am one step closer.

I become overwhelmed with this enormous energy that fills
me up, literally taking my breath away. A force much bigger and
greater than me is pulling me along—I am being carried. For once,
I am not resisting and fighting what is. Resisting comes naturally
to me, surrendering is what took great effort. I never imagined
feeling such elation as I float through time and enjoy what's given
to me.

8/7/09

Challenge: Fight the addiction of approval from others. The only approval you need is from God.

I have continued to pray strongly about Stanton and our relationship. I know Jesus has been assisting me because I gave Him permission to do so. Regardless of the trust I have in God, there's no denying that I still had my doubts along the way. Having said that, one thing is for certain: my heart always told me that Stanton and I are connected on a very deep level. Our love and respect for each other is quite obvious. It was my head that was getting in the way—my fears, doubts and the opinions of others. Do you know how disheartening it is when you finally find what you have always been looking for, but people around you tell you otherwise? I listened to people describe Stanton in one way, which I must admit, was accurate. I would question Stanton, but he never denied the truth, he simply said, "Yes, that was me. Ask me anything you want to know. I am not proud of some of my behavior, but it is what it is. I have lived a damn good life, and I won't make any apologies for it." I love that about him! He makes no excuses—you get what you get! I am so thankful I had the patience and open mind to go beyond what he was presenting to others. Behind the big, bold side of Stanton, I was discovering a man who has the most beautiful and loving soul, and there is so much more to him than he allows most people to see. The truth is, with me, he is a sensitive, thoughtful, sweet, caring, nurturing and loving man. He not only expresses his thoughts and emotions to me, but he *shows me his feelings.*

As much as I am ashamed to admit it, I suffered greatly from an addiction for approval. I would consume myself with trying to please everyone—trying to meet *their needs* and *their expectations*—and, in doing so, *I would lose sight of my own needs* and deny myself happiness. In my heart, I knew that Sweet Jesus was giving me the opportunity to face my fear—I was going to have to fight the addiction of approval from others. It would teach me to *learn to respect and value my own opinion* in order to discover and win the true love I have always wished for.

8/10/09

Prayer: Sweet Jesus, I pray that I am receptive to Your response. Most importantly, I need to trust Your response even when it is not in line with what I think it should be.

Although it may appear to others I am rushing into a relationship, I remind myself of what I literally begged for during prayer. "Jesus, please, please, please do not put me out in the dating scene. You know I am not a serial dater, nor do I enjoy juggling multiple men in casual relationships—it's just not my style. I would rather be single and enjoy my life with my girls, family and friends and focus on my career until the time is right. I am not looking for dinner dates, entertainment, fancy gifts or free vacations. I want a partner to enjoy life with, to travel with, to share business ideas with and to learn from. I want a man who loves like I love, a person who loves with all they have from within, someone who gives and receives openly. Someone who will value our relationship, respect us, cherish us and be loyal to our partnership even when faced with temptation. I want a strong man, just as I am a strong woman—I am not referring to strength in a physical way, but strength that is from within, true inner strength which is needed to help you rise above your circumstances."

As some people say, be careful for what you pray for. I admit, at times, I wanted to retract my prayer of being in a committed relationship and I thought, "Should I try dating other men?" This is not because I was not completely thrilled with Stanton, but once again, opinions of others started clouding my own beliefs. Friends and family would tell me I should date around, and that after a divorce, I should experience many other people, have fun, be single and play the field. Maybe this is my time to explore, be carefree, date around and not have to answer to anyone. I could make all of the decisions and simply do as I please. Wow, it did sound pretty enticing! As I let others influence me, I would begin to withdraw from Stanton. Although he loves me, he was also mindful of my circumstances. He often expressed to me his fear of meeting me too soon after my divorce, and that I might regret a missed opportunity to date around. He did not want to be my rebound. After several attempts to pull my heart away from him, I truly felt an ache and sadness inside, not the liberating freedom others told me I would feel. I questioned, "What am I doing? Why would I walk away from someone who gives and shares in such great happiness? Isn't this what I've always wanted? What if this turns out to be the missed opportunity? What if, by listening to others, I miss out on the greatest love that I could ever find." Once again, I needed to trust God. I remembered what the priest said in church, "There are no coincidences!"

As I sat in confusion, wanting to follow my heart, yet also be wise in my life choices, I asked Jesus, "Is it too soon for me to be in a relationship? Should I wait longer?" He responded gently and with sincerity in His voice, "You have waited long enough." With those words spoken, I began to softly cry. I knew exactly what He meant—although my divorce had recently been finalized, the love that I longed for had been missing for a lifetime.

8/11/09

Lesson: Embrace differences.

The past four months with Stanton have been amazing! It has been an incredible learning experience, and it is by far the healthiest relationship I have ever had. I am not suggesting that we have not faced hurdles, nor do I believe that we will ever be exempt from challenges or disagreements. What I have learned is that we have already started to prove to each other, *together* we can endure what comes our way.

Love passionately, stand up to your beliefs, but, in the end, respect each others views. What gives someone the right to think less of you just because they have a different opinion? Embrace differences!

8/13/09

Goal: Make your way up, God's Way.

I frequently run at Pontiff Park near my home. The running track surrounds a field used for soccer, baseball and football, and it rests beyond a cluster of bleachers. As I was approaching the track yesterday, I received another unusually powerful sense of the Holy Spirit being poured into me. It felt like I was connected to a hose, and I was being inflated to the maximum capacity. I feel a huge sense of fullness and warmth all over my body, and an enormous sense of emotion stirs inside of my being. It is almost so large at times that I feel like I can't breath because I'm so elated and lifted in spirit. The emotion that came over me yesterday is the exact feeling I've had in the past, and in the very same location of the park. This very distinct feeling tells me that something significant is happening, and I understand this energy will carry me to my destination. I cry tears of pure raw emotion, gratitude and honor. I have no doubt it is anything other than God's presence because the sense of love that washes over me is so unbelievably large I can only equate it to the enormity of God. Without words being spoken from my lips, I tell God that I acknowledge His presence and that I accept what He has planned for me—even though I don't know exactly what it is.

8/18/09

Prayer: Sweet Jesus, I want to know what love is. I want You to show me.

As summer comes to an end, I'm reminded of something I'd been promised—I recall randomly hearing in my heart, "Summer Lovin'" from the movie *Grease*. At the time, I laughed and asked sarcastically, "Ohhhhh, J.C., that's really funny! What? Are you trying to tell me I'll find love this summer?" The thought was humorous, and I thought I must be way off the mark with this message. Now, I realize I "heard" correctly, and Jesus was giving me another clue. Summer lovin' was definitely coming my way!

    Stanton and I met for a long weekend in Clearwater, Florida. We strolled along the sunny beach at The Carlouel with no one else in sight. We sat at water's break, completely comfortable in silence, staring out into the open sea, simply allowing ourselves to just be. I thought about how refreshing it is to be with a man who can relax and enjoy the moment, doing nothing but sitting next to me on a beautiful day. As the temperature began to rise from the heat of the glowing sun, we slowly made our way into the water to cool down. We would swim freely, and slowly make our way back to each other to meet in an embrace. We hugged each other tenderly and kissed softly, and I felt such immense joy! At the same time, I felt disbelief—someone was loving me in the exact way that I had always envisioned it would be. I felt a dream turning into reality.

    From out of the blue, we suddenly noticed a boat appear and it felt as if it was following us. The boat slowly made its way closer and closer to us—watching this young family head straight in our direction. Quickly it spun around to a stop—the name of the boat, which was now staring us directly in the face was, "Meant to

Be!" The family dropped anchor, and they began to play music, filling the silent ocean with laughter and kids playfully jumping out of the boat to swim. Stanton and I look at each other, and we burst out into laughter, in unison we exclaimed "No way!" The timing was too perfect! Stanton looked at me, his mouth agape, "Tell me this is not an obvious sign! What are the chances of this boat with that name dropping anchor right in front of us, especially when they have a completely open sea to themselves!" I laughed in agreement knowing all too well how God works in His perfect timing. I smiled from ear to ear at what *He was showing us—a glimpse of our future!* All I could feel inside was simply, "God, I love when you show off!!"

The laughter eventually fades, and my heart races to what Stanton always tells me, "Katie, we are *meant to be!*" Again, I remind myself, "There are *no coincidences.*"

8/19/09

Gift: EXPERIENCE the reality of God.

Today, I pray my journal will ignite a fire in lukewarm souls, offer hope to those who are suffering, and open the eyes of those who are spiritually blind. I pray that I can show others, through my experience, the *reality of God* and the *Spirit of Jesus Christ*—His love, His compassion, His understanding, His friendship, His beautiful peace that He so graciously wants to share and His amazing sense of humor. I would like to share a new kind of reality show!

9/2/09

Wisdom: Share the love that you hold within before it spoils and
time comes to an end.

Relish the days you are given, for you never know when it's your
last. Live as if there is no tomorrow, letting go of all of the pain in
your past. Cherish special memories, for they are built to last.
Focus not on what tomorrow will bring, but rather on what can be
learned and experienced today. Allow your soul to sing and delight
in all who come your way. The slightest smile can make
someone's day. Share the love you hold from within, before it
spoils and time comes to an end. I love you, Jesus.

9/10/09

PERSEVERANCE

As I crawled out of bed this morning, still crippled with fatigue from yesterday's long work day, I heard Jesus whisper one word, "Perseverance." Got it! Today, I am going to pray to the Holy Spirit to help me persevere. I am a fighter, and fighters do not give up.

Suddenly, I receive a message. In my heart, I see myself standing outside of a boxing ring, and I hear a bell ring. I am wearing a white, silk robe with my name written across the back in a beautiful shade of lilac. I'm bouncing up and down on my feet, warming up as I prepare to step inside the boxing ring. Jesus is my Coach, and we are standing together. He turns me to face Him and we both squat down—His hands are on His knees, and He is looking me directly in the eyes as He begins to give me advice and direction. We stand back up, and He rubs my shoulders to help me release tension. He speaks words of encouragement, and He tells me, "The fight is on." I hear the theme song from Rocky begin to play, which made me kind of laugh. I smiled and enthusiastically said, "Okay, I am ready for round one!"

All of sudden, my laughter and my excitement fade as I begin to question in confusion, "Wait. Jesus, what am I fighting?"

I hear no response.

9/27/09

"Trust in the Lord with all of your heart and lean not on your own understanding."

–Proverbs 3:5

Where do I even begin?

On my last journal entry, I wrote about Jesus preparing me for a fight. When I asked Him what I was fighting, I heard no response. I was confused with this vision because I felt so much peace in my life. I didn't feel any adversity, and it seemed as if I was just sailing along. After I finished my prayers and wrote in my journal that morning, I went upstairs, got dressed and finished packing—I flew to Houston that morning. I was meeting with clients that week, and Stanton and I had plans to go to the opening Texan's game. I went about my workday, but I was feeling unusually tired. That night, before going to bed, I had a terrible hot flash, broke out into a cold sweat, and felt extremely dizzy. I passed it off as possibly having a touch of a virus of some sort, and I went to sleep.

On September 11, 2009, which was the following day, I woke up feeling better. Realizing it was 9/11, I said a prayer for all of the victims and families that suffered loss and injury from the attack on our nation. I ate my breakfast and off to work I went. I had an appointment at 9:00 a.m. and I was meeting my client at her home before we drove to her family ranch that I am decorating. As we stood in her kitchen, I started feeling really sick again. I was in mid-conversation when all of a sudden a terrible hot flash, followed by a cold sweat, and a violent wave of nausea came washing over me. My head was spinning. I felt like I was going to pass out. I excused myself and ran to the restroom to re-group. My stomach was absolutely killing me, and I felt so strange and not present. I thought I had a stomach virus or food poisoning. Straightening myself up, I thought about going home, but I changed my mind. It is typical of me to want to keep moving forward. All day, I knew something was off as I could not shake the feeling of being completely off—it felt like I was zoning in and out of consciousness. Somehow, I made it through the workday.

After work, I met Stanton. We decided to go out to dinner and take it easy since I was feeling so poorly. We ate quickly at Carrabba's on Kirby and drove to Stanton's apartment afterward. As we were holding hands, walking through the parking lot, I suddenly heard, in my heart, "This is gonna' hurt." Immediately, I thought, "What? This is gonna' hurt? Jesus, is that You? What do You mean?" I heard no response. I dismissed it. In my mind, I told myself, "I am not going to acknowledge that comment. It sounds frightening!" Immediately, I heard it again, "This is gonna' hurt." I began to question what I was hearing—I really thought my mind was trying to deceive me. Again, I didn't want to acknowledge the message because I didn't want to draw on or create negative energy. I decided not to tell Stanton what I heard, fearing that if I spoke it, I would will it my way. I firmly decided that I was not going into a negative mindset.

I woke up at 1:00 a.m. in absolutely excruciating pain. I ran to the bathroom, staggering along the way, disoriented and barely able to stand on my feet. I was bleeding profusely, sweating and my head was spinning until I quickly passed out. When I woke up, I was laying on the floor of the bathroom—my body was shaking and convulsing as if I was having a seizure. I saw blood all over my body and all over the floor. I tried to call out to Stanton, but I couldn't speak—in my mind, I slowly repeated, "Help. Help. Help." I eventually managed to pick myself up off of the floor, only to be taken down again by another huge wave of sickness attacking me. This time when I passed out, I hit my mouth on a door knob in front of me, eventually falling to the floor so hard the noise woke up Stanton. Apparently, he found me unconscious on the floor with blood streaming out of my nose, mouth and a puddle on the floor. I recall him standing over me, fearfully calling out my name, "Katie! Katie! Katie!" I wanted to respond to him, but I still couldn't speak. He picked me up off of the floor, trying to ask me what happened—I could barely murmur, "I don't know. Something is wrong." He was trying to clean me up when I passed out again, thankfully, this time in his arms. He set me back down on the floor, and he ran to the phone, frantically calling 9-1-1.

I arrived at the Methodist Hospital emergency room and I could see and feel the nervous energy of the staff and doctors rushing around my room, shouting orders out frantically to one another. More and more people entered my room and that made me recognize the severity of my condition. Stanton was in the mix, squeezing his way to be by my side, telling me how much he loved me, and he spoke words of encouragement as he held my hand. I could see tears welling up in his eyes, and the look of concern on his face told me again my health was in trouble. I specifically remember lying in the hospital bed, feeling a "crash" coming on, and the only thing I knew I could do was to focus on Jesus. In my heart, I called out to Him repeatedly, in firm confidence, "Jesus! Jesus! Jesus!" I knew He was with me. I knew He would help me. I knew this incident would have a purpose. I knew this was a great opportunity to trust Him with my life.

I was bleeding internally, but the doctors could not locate the source of the bleed. I was rushed to ICU where I had a continuous stream of blood transfusions. In the most excruciating moments, I repeated the words that I had been taught, "Jesus, I trust in You. Jesus, I trust in You. Jesus, I trust in You." Lying helplessly in my bed, surrounded by doctors and nurses, a vision came to my heart—Jesus was standing over me in silence, dressed in his white robe (unlike how I usually see Him). His hands were raised over my belly, and His eyes were peacefully closed. Although I could not see them, I knew His powerful healing rays were penetrating me and repairing the source of my bleed. Although this image did not relieve me from feeling pain, it removed my fearful thoughts of dying. I was confident I would be okay.

When the pain was more than I could bear, I would meditate on Jesus's crucifixion. I would ask Him, as I often did, "How did You do it? How did You manage your pain? I am not as strong as You. Help me, this hurts so much. I am totally depleted, and I am suffering terribly. I am on my last leg and, I can't take anymore.

Please, have mercy on me. Heal me." I finally fell asleep in my misery. That night, as I was sleeping, I felt my room completely surrounded with angels—they were everywhere! I could literally feel their spirits hovering over my bed. I remember thinking to myself, "Oh my, God! Look how many people are watching over me!" I simply could not believe the magnitude of angels that were with me. I could not see faces or bodies—it was just like a round, white glowing presence, but instinctively I knew exactly how to identify what I was seeing. I remember recognizing the spirit of a dear friend of mine, Jo Beth Nelson. She had passed away when we were in high school after she fought a long battle with cystic fibrosis. I specifically recall acknowledging her presence by telling her, "Jo Beth, I can see you." I woke up several times throughout the night, and every time I woke up I was muttering, "Trust in the Lord with all of your heart, and lean not on your own understanding." As I have mentioned before, I am *not* one to know or repeat scripture, which is why I knew it was Jesus prompting my soul. Regardless, I knew I had read it before, and I looked it up yesterday—it is Proverbs 3:5. I concluded that my hospitalization was serving a purpose beyond my own understanding. Again, I was to trust Jesus, learn from this experience, and understand that in the end, it would somehow be beneficial. I fell back to sleep.

The very next morning, just as I was waking from the night, a nurse came in my room with a phone in her hand. She told me a friend of mine was on the line, her name was Joanna. Yes, it was Joanna Nelson, Jo Beth's mother, the mother of my dear friend who had passed away, my friend whose spirit had just been with me during the night! I had not spoken to Joanna in years! She heard about my hospitalization through a friend of mine, and she said that she felt "Beth" *urging* her to call me. She also said that she hesitated to call since it had been so long since we had last spoken. She added that Beth's urging was so strong that she could not ignore her request. Once again, God was giving me confirmation that what I was experiencing was real, and to leave no room for doubt. I am so grateful to know that Jo Beth is one of my guardian angels!

9/28/09

Meditate: Find and focus on anything positive that can result from times of suffering. Utilize it to build your strength and character. Overcome adversity.

During my hospitalization, I tried to focus on the positive things that were coming from my suffering. My very first thought was Stanton. This was an opportunity for him to not only show me, but my friends and family the dedication and beauty that I knew his heart held. I also realized it was a great opportunity for us to be reassured in just how strong our love is. I specifically recall early in our courtship Stanton telling me he had my best interest at heart and how much he truly loves me. He told me that if I wanted to really know who he is that I needed to watch the movie, *The Notebook*. He added, "That man in the movie is me. I am the man who truly loves you, and I will always care for you and protect you. If you are ever sick, I am the man who would never leave your side." Well, this was Stanton's chance to put his words to action.

Stanton never left my side. He was with me every single day and every single night—he only went home to shower and change his clothes. He sat at the side of my bed, slept in a chair next to me and held my hand day in and day out. He whispered words of love and encouragement, prayed with me, took charge and stayed on top of all of the doctors and nurses. He took notes on the test results, followed up by getting second and third opinions, and kept my family and friends updated with the latest reports. I can't even begin to tell you how many doctors and nurses came in my room, telling me, "That man loves you!" One of my doctors told me Stanton ran to catch him in the hall before he entered my room.

Stanton began to cry to him, "Please save her. It has taken me forty years to find her. I can't lose her now."

In addition to focusing on the positive outcomes of my suffering, I was also focused on one word: humble. This was an excellent opportunity to let go of any pride I had. Pride is one of the seven deadly sins, and true love can't exist in its presence. The opposite of pride is humility. I couldn't help but humble myself. When you are bleeding internally, you are exposed. I will spare you the details, but just know there is nothing pretty to see or smell. Stanton was there for *everything*, and he never flinched—he actually withstood the unpleasantries better than I did!

As far as outward appearances go, I am typically a gal who maintains herself. I rarely leave the house without a swipe of blush on my cheeks, gloss on my lips and my hair fresh and clean. Let me tell you, while I was in the hospital, I went five days without having my hair washed! Let me add one more thing, I have extra fine hair! Hot flashes, cold sweats, I.V. drips and hospital garb do not help this already poor situation. My blonde hair was literally, *dirty* blonde. My face was very swollen from all of the blood transfusions and medications. I had a heat rash all over the left side of my face, a black eye and a busted and swollen lip from my fall. I was not even close to being shiny, pink and rosy; I was dull, white and green. Despite my appearance, Stanton *still* looked me directly in my swollen eyes, softly brushed my dirty hair away from my oily, pale face, and told me how beautiful I am and how very much he loves me. During our courtship, he would tell me daily, "Katie, you are so beautiful to me, but it is your *heart* that I truly love." Stanton's actions backed up his words! Sweet Jesus always told me, "Listen not so much as to what they say, watch what they do. Consistency in behavior and performance over time, this will be your truth."

Humble. I knew I had officially gotten over my "self" when, by week's end, I was actually *comfortable* conversing with cute, young residents and doctors as I sat on my throne, aka, potty as I was still bleeding internally. Yes, humble!

Two nurses, who were my "beauty angels," finally came to my rescue! I specifically remember Nurse Janice walking into my room—she looked so beautiful with her clean, styled, shiny hair and light fresh makeup. I got a whiff of her perfume that smelled as sweet as a garden. I instantly thought to myself, "Ohhhh, I miss that!" I think she took one look at me in the bed and thought, *Wow! This girl needs help!* Before I could say anything, she quickly left the room, only to reappear with her friend, Valvina. They were equipped with water buckets, shampoo, conditioner, a hair dryer and my round brush. Amen! All I could say was, "Thank you, Sweet Jesus!" Like I said, He sure knows how to read my mind! Miraculously, I was transformed in ICU! The doctors who had been caring for me barely recognized me when they returned to my room. I still laugh at the thought of them looking at their transformed patient—it was as if they had just seen a ghost. When Stanton entered the room and saw me he excitedly exclaimed, "She's back!" He looked over at the doctors standing next to me and jokingly said, "I told you she's beautiful!" We all laughed!

I remained in ICU for six days until I was stable enough to be transferred to a regular room. There I stayed for an additional four days. I lost a total of 17 units of blood, which is equivalent to a body and a half. After CAT scans, MRIs, angiograms, an upper endoscope, two colonoscopies, two red tag blood tests and a Meckles scan, the doctors were never able to locate the source of the bleeding. It had stopped on its own, and I was finally released from the hospital. Again, my heart immediately returns to Jesus standing over me with His hands raised above my belly, healing what needed to be fixed.

9/29/09

WISDOM: Do not wait for challenging and frightening moments
to recognize what we should cherish every single day.

I continue to hear Jesus whisper to my heart, "Rely not on your
own understanding." I interpret this to mean acceptance of what is,
acceptance of the greater force that surrounds you, acceptance and
willingness to allow that force to carry you to your destination.
Experiencing God, not just praying to God but truly feeling God—
inviting Him into your life, respecting Him, loving Him and
learning from the challenges we face.

I truly believe God arranged my meeting with Stanton. I
believe that even though I knew and felt this in my heart, I still had
humanly doubts. It is natural for us to question what is and to also
question what is not. I believe God wanted to remove any bit of
lingering doubt, from both of us. He utilized my hospitalization to
show each of us the fragility of life, and to cherish the genuine love
we have for each other. I often wonder why it takes frightening
moments to recognize what we should already recognize and
cherish every day.

Stanton's consistent actions continue to show me his love is
genuine and true. Again, I do not assume or expect our relationship
to be exempt from challenges and hardships. I know that we will
not be perfect in our relationship—we are human and we are
bound to make mistakes. I do not believe we are special because
God introduced us in a unique way—I believe we were *both open*
to give and receive love. God simply showed us the way. I believe
that *together*, we will persevere and endure what comes our way,
and we will cherish the *gift of love*.

10/1/09

Prayer: Sweet Jesus, I pray for all of the sick members of our community and for their caretakers. Strengthen their spirit with Your overwhelming love.

When I was sick in the hospital, I promised Jesus that everyday I would pray not only for the sick members of our community, but also for the family members and caretakers. I have seen and experienced the weight, both physically and emotionally, that a caregiver bears. I assist and watch my mother care for my father. He is physically unable to do so for himself. Now, after being a patient in the hospital, I had the opportunity to experience the other side—the physical pain that comes with illness and the emotional toll that can tax the mind. When you are sick, you have to depend on others. I realized that illness is hard, no matter what side of the bed you are on—the sick feel the pain and frustration of not being well, independent and free. Caretakers struggle watching their loved one suffer, and they too lose their freedom in life, as they once knew it. Life revolves around hospitals, rehabilitation, doctors visits, tending to their loved one and a lot of waiting— waiting on doctors for test results, referrals, answers to questions and waiting for cures to be found before it's too late. Patience is required. Hope is needed.

When I reflect on what I have been through, I know it is so tiny in comparison to what others experience. I feel my heart ache for all of those who suffer. I wish I could make it stop.

Heavenly Father, in the name of your precious Son, Jesus, I pray that those who are suffering invite You into their life and that they allow themselves to open their heart and soul to You. Although the physical pain may not dissipate, the heart can remain healthy in Your love and peace. Amen.

10/2/09

Thanksgiving: Sweet Jesus, I am grateful for my life!

As I sit in the Adoration Chapel today, I am simply thankful for sitting here!

I have been doing a Beth Moore Bible study, *John, 90 Days with the Beloved Disciple*, and I could not help but to take notice of the perfect timing and the parallel to my life at this time. As you know, I have been recounting my experience with internal bleeding, the need for blood transfusions and my hospitalization. Knowing in my heart God always has a purpose, I read Beth's brilliant message. She writes, "The joy of Jesus comes to the believer only one way: transfusion. Like an intravenous drip from vine to branch!" I choose to believe that I was transfused with seventeen units of God's love and mercy! Thank You, Sweet Jesus!

10/5/09

Happiness: I am on God's Way!

This past weekend I went to Shreveport, Louisiana to meet Stanton's family and friends. They were so welcoming. It was easy to see the strong bonds of friendship that Stanton established at an early age.

Stanton drove me around Shreveport to give me the grand tour. We had rolled down the windows and opened the sunroof in his car to optimize the beautiful day! Soon enough, Michael Jackson's tune, "Rock With You" came on the radio—I turned up the volume, smiled in complete joy, and I felt excitement brewing from deep within. I turned to look at Stanton, and I was suddenly filled with more joy. Joy in knowing that I listened to God's direction. Joy in knowing that I not only listened, but that I trusted Him enough to follow. Joy in knowing that God led me to true love.

As we continue to ride around we came across a little, rundown shopping strip. I immediately notice the sign on the corner. It read, "God's Way." Can you believe? I smiled from ear to ear, knowing in my heart that God has shown me, yet again, that I am on His path. The only path I want to be on. The path I dreamt of several months ago, *God's Way*, and Stanton is sitting next to me, smiling and enjoying the ride!

10/13/09

Challenge: Grow in all areas of your life.

Stanton and I went to Florida this past weekend so I could meet his mother, Susan. She greeted us at the airport, and when Stanton saw her he had a big, sweet smile on his face. His arms were wide open as he prepared for a warm, tight embrace from her. He always speaks so highly of her, and their comfortable body language told me why. She was just as beautiful and sweet in person as I had imagined her to be. I was also drawn to Susan's spirituality, strong faith and openness—I am always thrilled to meet someone who can relate to all of the amazing energy that the Holy Spirit brings forth, and it was fun for us to share our experiences. I was also drawn to the relationship Susan shared with Stanton. I love their easygoing and casual conversations, and the way they just simply hang out together. Nothing was forced. As for me, it certainly did not feel like a first-time meeting. Rather it felt like a beautiful reunion. Once again, I realize how natural everything is when it comes to Stanton.

We enjoyed our visit by dining at The Palm Pavilion with his amazingly sweet and welcoming family that owns this historical landmark. Stanton and I relaxed and took many strolls down the beach. We reflected on how much our relationship had grown in the short six months we have been together. We agreed that it felt as if we had been together for a lifetime. We have a connection and energy that is so overwhelmingly strong and deep, a feeling that neither one of us had ever experienced before, a feeling that can only be described by two simple words, soul mates.

10/19/09

Prayer: Sweet Jesus, I hope to softly encourage others to go beyond their dream of having beautiful and peaceful rooms. I wish for people to dream of a beautiful and peaceful soul.

My ultimate dream is to infuse spirituality into the world, but in a new, modern and fun way. At the same time, I aim to respect tradition and values. I want peace and love for humanity.

I recently started a blog on my website. I am hoping to utilize it not only as a way for others to view my interior design work, but also as a means to softly encourage others to go beyond having beautiful and peaceful rooms. I wish for people to also dream of having a peaceful and beautiful soul.

A talented, and highly sought after blogger, Joni Webb of *Cote de Texas*, saw my recent interior design work published in *Papercity* magazine. She wrote about my work on October 15, 2009. I was touched and surprised to see Joni's beautifully written words describing my interior design style and my spirituality, and her readers echoed her thoughts. I realize that my design talent is not my focus, and what impressed me the most was that readers were drawn to my *spirituality*. What I recognize is not the need for "another" interior designer, but the need for spirituality. This is the key that brings peace not only to the home, but also to the soul.

10/27/09

Meditate: Sweet Jesus, how beautiful to see You through the
eyes of faith.

I was in Houston this past week for work, and of course, to spend
time with Stanton! On Sunday, we attended mass at St. Anne's
Church—standing with the rest of the congregation, I began to
receive the same strong sense of Spirit wrapping around me. Once
again, the feeling told me God has me on a mission, and I felt very
overwhelmed! The feeling is so grand tears began to roll down my
cheeks. Not wanting anyone to see me cry, I wiped the tears away
as fast as I could, but they continued to come flooding down
uncontrollably. My skin was stinging, my chest expanding, and
I was filled with warmth. I questioned myself and got upset for
feeling as if I am someone important. In my mind I say, "Who do
you think you are? Why would God choose you? What a conceited
thought!" I wonder if I am just being egotistical or having
delusions of grandeur, but the feeling is so real that no amount of
doubt could invalidate what I felt in spirit. In my heart, I
acknowledged my feelings to Jesus. I told Him that I am aware of
His presence. I expressed to Him that I am open to receive Him,
and I am ready for whatever He presents to me. As I write this,
I almost hate to record what I feel—I sound full of myself, and
I despise it, but if I didn't write it down, the feelings described
would not be complete or truthful.

I want to run out of the church so I can breath and pull myself
together, but the liturgy begins. It is about Bartimaeus, a man who
is blind. He hears Jesus out on the streets and cries out to Him
loudly, asking to be healed. People around him are annoyed with
his behavior and try to silence him. He cries out again, begging
Jesus for help. He can't see Him, but his faith tells him He is a

healer. Jesus stops in the crowd and calls the man over. He commends Bartimaeus for recognizing who He is with his *eyes of faith* and, He grants him sight. Asking for and receiving sight is a true act of bravery for Bartimaeus. He can no longer make his living by begging on the streets, and he is exposed to surroundings that he has never seen. It would be uncomfortable. My heart recognizes that he thought it was amazingly beautiful!

I can relate to Bartimaeus. I see my past, being spiritually blind, crying out for help and begging Jesus for mercy. I imagine myself living back in the day, and I am out in the blazing heat among a large, loud crowd of people—I am determined to see and reach Jesus, but I stay silent, unable to speak for some reason. As He walks in front of me, I aggressively stretch my arms out as far as they could possibly extend, and my fingertips just barely catch the edge of His robe. I grab the robe and latch on so tight that He stops and turns to look at who is pulling on His clothing. I am met with His warm and perspiring face. He speaks no words, and His solemn expression does not change yet He gently picks up my hand and safely leads me out of the crowd. I follow Him gratefully, knowing that what I have just chosen to do is surrender my life to God, and to live a new life, following Jesus. I would be exposed to a new way of living, and it may be uncomfortable at times. But, my guess is that it will be amazingly beautiful!

I look up at Stanton standing next to me. He sweetly turns to catch my gaze and he looks directly into my eyes. He gently lifts my hand, squeezes it tightly and smiles at me lovingly.

10/30/09

Challenge: Offer your fear of failure to God. Instill the hope of success. Find ways to work smarter, not harder.

Last night, fear was raging in my mind. Don't get me wrong, I am blessed to have jobs in this economy, but I am still struggling with so many financial responsibilities as a single parent. I get frustrated thinking about it, and I wonder, "How am I ever going to get ahead? Please show me. I am begging you to teach me how to delegate, manage and produce in the most efficient way. Please share your wisdom with me. I need your guidance so that I can provide for my family."

Heavenly Father, in the name of Jesus, I offer my fear of failure to You. Instill in me the hope of success. Show me ways to work smarter, not harder. Not only do I need for You to provide me with great opportunities, but I also need You to prepare me for the opportunities that come my way. I am listening. Thank You so much for your help! I love You, always!

Aggghhhhhh, I feel better already…

10/31/09

I AM ALWAYS WITH YOU, WHEREVER YOU ARE.

I have not been running since my internal bleed. It completely zapped me of my strength and energy. I am excited because I finally feel replenished and ready to go again! The weather is beautiful today—the sun is shining brightly, it is 73 degrees, and a cool, crisp breeze is gently racing across the way. It is time to get myself back out on the track. I went upstairs in a hurry, not wanting to waste any precious time, and I quickly throw on my Nike gear. I bounced happily back down the stairs so I could do something that I love so much, running with Jesus.

Yesterday, I was staring at the stack of medical bills that have grown on my desk. Uuughhhh, more to add to my already existing large load. I could not help but feel disappointment. I knew I needed a pep talk. As I walked out the side door, I stumbled upon a pink tennis ball that my girls had been playing with. I picked it up so no one would trip—I looked at the ball in my hand and I saw the word, "Hope" written on one side. I looked intently and thought to myself, "Yes, hope! There is always hope!" Although I did not trip on the ball, I did stumble. I stumbled upon inspiration, HOPE! It brought a smile to my face.

As I smiled with *hope*, I continued walking down the driveway. Soon enough, I heard Jesus speak loudly, and he sounded excited, "Finally!" I smiled even broader when I saw Him waiting for me, and I began to laugh. I instantly had a flash back— I remember lying in the hospital bed just a few short weeks ago, and I would meditate on our runs together, wondering if we would ever have them again. I missed *our time* in the sunshine. I remember thinking about how appreciative I was going to be if I could run again. I thanked Sweet Jesus and told Him how much I needed Him. He replied, "I am always with you, wherever you are." I responded, " I know You are because I can feel Your precious Spirit with me!" I shared with Him, once again, my appreciation for all of His help, and I reminded Him how very much I depend on Him for all of my needs. He smiled.

We arrived at the park and we started our run at a nice, slow pace. Usually, Jesus runs ahead of me as I follow, but today He ran next to me—He simply said, "I know you need Me as close to you as possible." I am here to tell you, the Man can read a mind like no other! I had been feeling so vulnerable the past two days, and I just needed to feel His protection and hear His sounding voice. I thought to myself as we ran, "I am so blessed!"

We ran in synch, and Sade began to sing, "Your Love Is King." I smiled and spoke to Jesus, "If I could sing, I would sing this song to You, but as You know, singing is *not* one of my God-given talents! Instead, I will let Sade do the honors—just know this is how I feel about You." We laughed, and the words began to sing soulfully, "Your love is king. Crown you with my heart. Your love is king. Never need to part...touching the very part of me. It's making my soul sing. Taking the very heart of me. I am crying out for more..."

I soon heard Jesus say, "Don't stop!"

11/3/09

Lesson: Live life as if it is game time! In order to play effectively you have to forget the mistakes you have made and the embarrassment that comes along with it. You must humble yourself and move forward.

All day the city of New Orleans was busy preparing for the Saints' game. Due to our winning season, many local businesses were shut down. Fans were busy making their preparations for game day parties. You would have thought it was Christmas day. The only difference was that the city was not flashing in red and green—the city sparkled in black and gold! The streets were very busy, and the grocery stores were packed. The checkout lines were as long as a hurricane evacuation line as people stocked up on game day fare. Everybody knows the loyalty of a Saints fan and today was no exception. Go, Drew Brees and team!

Victory! Other than our big win against the Falcons there was another special moment for me during game time. I felt as if it was Jesus, my Coach, speaking directly to me, through one of the sports commentators—he said that a quarterback has to have amnesia because in order to play effectively you have to forget the mistakes you make and the embarrassment that comes along with it. You must humble yourself and move on. I see such wisdom in that statement, and I believe that it is a lesson we should apply to all areas of life.

11/11/09

Lesson: God knows each of us so well that He will customize His form of communication in a way that He knows you can understand, but you must be open to receive it. Put forth the effort!

I have been reflecting on people's responses and reactions when I share my personal experience with Jesus. I find that people are either inspired or completely turned off. When I mention that I "hear" God's prompting in certain area's of my life, some respond by saying, "I pray to God everyday, and I never hear Him speak to me! Why does He talk to you? Why not me?." I also share my stories of what I believe to be blessings, answers to my prayers. The response is typically, "I have been praying to God about a particular situation and nothing has happened or changed. Prayers don't work for me." I have also commented to others that I find God to have a funny sense of humor. One response I received was "I think God has a bad sense of humor. What's so funny about the pain and suffering He causes?"

I find interest in seeing how life can be perceived so differently. As strong as my belief is, I never frown upon anyone who lacks faith. I ask myself, "What if I was not raised by parents who taught me the importance of faith? I would probably believe the exact opposite. Furthermore, I don't want my faith taken away from me, nor do I want someone to tell me that I can't believe in God. So then, why would I frown upon someone else with an opposing belief? Why would I *not* like someone for not believing in God?" We all have the power to choose. But, we also have the power to share our perception.

When I do share my spiritual experiences with others, I can often see the expression on their face—it reads, "What is this girl talking about?" I have learned to embrace opinions, because that's all it is, an opinion. I look from their perspective, and I know that if I had not experienced the Holy Spirit, I would look at myself in the same crazy way. I would have a really hard time understanding or believing without a personal experience. The reason I continue to share the details of my relationship with God is that I know, in my heart, that my experiences are authentic. I know I can't prove it, but I know myself well enough to know that I would not conjure up these stories, nor is it in me to have the desire too! I do *not* take any comfort or pleasure in having others question me like I am delusional. I am not the one who takes comfort or pleasure in being looked at differently. I know some people thrive on that, but I am not one of them! It is truly a test for me because I would rather live in a way that is non-confrontational, but I choose otherwise because my love and belief in the existence of God and the spirit of Jesus is so amazingly strong, honest and genuine.

When people say, "I pray to God, and I never hear Him speak to me." My response would be, "How are you listening?" I think most of us believe the only way to hear God is if He shouts down from the sky. Most of us are so *literal* that we think speaking only comes from a mouth. I believe we are all "spoken to" differently because God knows each of us so well that He customizes His forms of communication in a way that He knows we will understand, but it is your responsibility to make the effort and discover that form. For me, it is through my senses—I was never able to grasp knowledge and understanding merely through reading a textbook or listening to the history of religion in class. This is why I never could relate to God by reading scripture in the Bible. My second question would be, "Are you paying attention?" You must be open to all forms of communication. It could be through music, art, nature, books, headlines, athletics and/or others speaking to you. Have you ever prayed to God about needing an answer, let's say for work, and "out of the blue" you run into someone who specializes in your profession and you connect. Poof, assistance is given! Do you think that's coincidence? He might speak through the voice of an innocent child. What about nature? Have you ever been praying to God, looking for answers or confirmation only to hear a thunderous roar in the sky? Or, see a flash of electric lightning burst through the air or the sun parts from behind a cloud to reveal itself, sending forth God's warmth and love to comfort you and brighten your day. Have you ever prayed about something and you hear an inner voice speak to your heart? The thought is not forced because you have silenced your mind—have you ever considered that the voice you heard could be God speaking to you?

"I have been praying to God, and nothing has changed or improved?" Have you ever considered that no answer is the answer? Have you ever thought the answer lies within your heart, yet *you are unwilling* to make the changes within yourself to answer your own prayer? Maybe, the answer to your prayer depends upon someone else making the changes within themselves in order for your prayer to be answered. God gives us the choice to choose for ourselves. Let's not forget about time. Often prayers are answered very clearly, but it takes time for the answer to be revealed. Are you being patient? God utilizes time on our behalf, preparing us for what lies ahead.

I don't understand why people get frustrated when they want answers from God, but they haven't put forth any effort. I know about this because it was a part of my routine for awhile. At times, people pray with absolutely no enthusiasm, no meaning. They simply recite memorized prayers without even thinking because the words are so *routine* that they roll off of your lips. Let me ask you, "Have you ever been in a relationship where only one person is willing to work and put forth any effort? Does it work? How can you expect God to work in your life when you are not willing to work with Him?" This may be why you don't hear God and why you think He does not answer prayers. It takes *two* willing, eager and participating partners. I believe God is no exception. *You* must put forth the effort.

I am certainly not an expert in this matter, and I have absolutely no formal training, educational background or masters degree in theology/religion or anything related, but I often reflect on why so many people question God and His ways. In many circumstances, I think we either don't realize or we just forget about the simple miracles of everyday life, and we only look to God in our times of suffering. It's especially hard to understand

God when we experience sorrow, grief, pain, illness, financial hardships and adversity in life. This is when people question if there really is a God. In times of tragedy people say, "If there is a God, why would He allow this to happen? If He can do anything like He says He can, why this?" I don't believe we will ever understand why certain tragedies unfold, and no matter how close you are to God, you are *not* exempt from pain, suffering and sorrow. What I do believe is that you can take comfort in Him during difficult times and ask for His help in healing the pain by taking solace in His unconditional love. I believe God wants to bring something greater than pain from suffering. The most beneficial thing we can do is give suffering a purpose. I think the best example is John Walsh from *America's Most Wanted*. This is a man who lost his young son to kidnapping and murder. The suffering and pain he feels is unimaginable to me, but what I do recognize is how he turned his tragedy into victory. He did not *personally* benefit from the loss of his son, but thousands of other children and families have. He can at least rejoice in knowing that through his pain, he found purpose. He honored his deceased son by saving hundreds of lives. He has reunited families, and he has spared them the loss, pain and suffering that he endures.

11/16/09

Meditate: Although I can't see all that God has planned for me, I can feel the glory in whatever it shall be.

I woke from a dream this past weekend. I could hear a voice with authority speaking to me—God told me that I am exactly where I am supposed to be in my life, and the timing is perfect. He told me to stay on the path, and I responded by saying, "Thank You!" in acknowledgement to His communication to me. I wondered if what I had just heard was really a message or if it was just a dream. I had such peace in my heart, which was my reminder that it is more than just a dream. God wanted to encourage me and give me thanks for listening, following and trusting in His direction.

I can't stop thanking Jesus. I am so grateful and appreciative because He gave me direction when I had none, He taught me how to trust Him, He showed me true love, and He gave me hope for a bright future. Although I can't see all that He has planned for me, I can feel the glory in whatever it shall be. I continue to pray to God that I never lose sight of the beauty to be found in each day. I pray to stay grounded in His presence, in His love and in His promise.

Today, I pray, "God, once again, I promise You that my number one goal is to maintain complete dependence on You and You alone. You are the way to my future. Thank You for guiding me and showing me all that You created me to be."

11/17/09

WE HAVE COME A LONG WAY IN A SHORT PERIOD OF TIME. DON'T STOP.

As I look into the eyes of Sweet Jesus, and meditate on the image of Divine Mercy, I hear Him speak, "We have come a long way in a short period of time. Don't stop." I feel His loving Spirit suddenly wash over me, and I return His love by acknowledging, accepting, welcoming and embracing the wave of emotion that I know to be Him.

11/26/09

Challenge: View each day as if it is your last. Take full advantage of opportunities before they pass.

Today I pray, "Sweet Jesus, I asked You to show me the way, and I opened myself up to Your Spirit and God's plans for me. I began to recognize all of the opportunities You regularly send my way. I view each day as if it were my last, taking full advantage of opportunities before they pass, exploring each moment as if it is a treasure waiting to be discovered; no stone is left unturned, and the path is stamped by my footprints in anticipation of the gifts You place before me. I keep my eyes wide open, never looking back, focused and straight forward I follow Jesus in His tracks, watching in awe the cross that goes before me—always in motion, balanced and steady, my reminder of His strength and His willingness to carry the weight for me."

12/2/09

Lesson: "To live with love you have to chance losing it."

I read an interview given to Brad Pitt in *Parade* magazine. I was captivated, and reminded of a very important lesson. Brad shares his wisdom. Brad asks the interviewer, "Do you know how to tell true love? It's when someone else's interests trumps your own. I like to put it that way: trumps your own. Love of somebody else—of family, of your kids—becomes the most important, most worthwhile thing in your life. It's what you foster and protect."

"You have to recognize real love when it's there," Pitt goes on, "and know that in going after it, there is always a risk. To live with love, you have to chance losing it. That's also true when you decide to have kids. It's the risk you take for love."

As Stanton and I are challenged by distance, time and the wake of what a divorce brings, I remind myself what true love is...a risk.

12/5/09

Challenge: Pray to God with a grateful heart even in the most sorrowful moments in life.

A woman has blessed me and her name is Mary Murphy. She came into my family's life years ago when my precious grandmother, Annette Shepherd, became ill. The priest at our church referred her to my family. She not only cared for Granny, she cared for all of us by blessing our home with her strong, loving spirit. Eventually, my grandmother passed away, but Mary was a permanent fixture in our life.

My mom started a very successful catering company called, The Best of Susan, after my father was incarcerated for twenty-one months back in 1992. From that event, we were all emotionally devastated, and we lost almost everything monetarily. My mother was desperate to support our young family. Fortunately, she recognized her gift from God, and it was time to put it to work! As my dad loves to say, "She is a magician in the kitchen!" and catering came into play. She needed help, so my grandfather, Alvin Shepherd, who lived in a garage apartment behind our home, gladly chipped in. Mary was right there with them—up to her elbows in food and dishes. I soon joined them as well, and what a collaboration it was! We all shared many laughs, many tears from the grueling work, and physical and emotional exhaustion but mostly an abundance of quality time shared together and fulfillment in watching others relish over my mother's creations.

I loved when Mary would sing her gospel music, which I frequently asked her to do. Her soul would immediately fill up the kitchen! I specifically remember one day in particular, we were all cooking and talking—the next thing I noticed was Mary throwing her hands up in the air, waving them from side to side, smiling with complete joy and belting out the tune, "I Can Fly," by R.J. Kelly. As trivial as it sounds, I can't begin to describe how significant this moment was—it resonated deep within me. At the time, I didn't know why. Looking back, I believe it was the example Mary was demonstrating—she was singing joyfully, living fully, always believing and trusting in God, even after a lifetime of hardships. She had just lost her husband, Murphy, to illness, and her son and daughter-in-law were killed in a car accident. Her other son had lost a leg in a non-related incident. She struggled financially, but she *always* found something to sing about.

Several years passed, and my grandfather, Alvin Shepherd, Gramps, became ill, and Mary cared for him until he passed away. Today, she has stepped in, once again and now she cares for my own father, David, as he fights to regain his speech and mobility following his cerebral hemorrhage.

Unfortunately, last week, Mary lost yet another son. Never one to sit still or wallow in self-pity, Mary still came to work. As she walked through the door, still standing strong, I embraced her with tears and a big warm hug. I asked, "How are you doing it, Mary?" She looked at me, than she looked up towards the sky and peacefully said, "I get in my bed at night, and I start praising God. I thank Him for all that I do have. I thank Him for this very moment. I thank Him for watching over me. I ask Him to give me His strength, and I call out to all of the angels, and I ask them for their protection." I burst into tears, hugging Mary tighter, knowing this is another example to follow. I pray that I have a grateful heart, even in the most sorrowful moments in life.

12/7/09

Meditate: "Walk in faith, not in fear."

12/8/09

Lesson: A house is not a HOME unless it is full in spirit, and not just full of furnishings.

I started a blog on my website three months ago. I questioned what I wanted to write about. It is an interior design website, so I should be writing according to the subject, but, I am disenchanted to a degree because hundreds of blogs already cover the subject of interior design. I question, "What more can I contribute to a subject that is extensively covered?" I thought about my true passion—my relationship with God, and His miraculous renovation skills.

I decided to incorporate all of the subjects I'm passionate about. Maybe, it can be more of an inspiration for a *lifestyle* of simplicity, peace and love—a traditional subject, presented in a modern way.

I decided to humble myself, readers or not, and I wrote about the most important foundation of interior design. I want to remind readers that no matter how famous, professional or talented your interior designer may be and no matter how much money you spend on furnishings, fabrics and accessories—you will not *truly* be peaceful in your home, until you find peace from within your soul. Do not misunderstand me—I am a firm believer that your surroundings and atmosphere create, set and influence the stage of emotions we want to feel, but it is simply not the answer to finding a lifetime of true inner peace and joy.

A house is not a home unless it is full in spirit—and not just full of furnishings.

12/10/09

Practice: Although your body and mind may want to fight and resist opposition that comes your way, consciously remove the negative emotions that are attached. Repeatedly tell your mind and body to accept the challenge so it loses power. Smile, and thank Jesus for the lesson you will learn.

I am working on developing a new habit—I like to call it my "Mary" habit. I am practicing thanking God, for every challenge that comes my way. I accept and embrace difficulty in anticipation of growing stronger. Although my mind and body want to fight and resist the opposition that comes my way, I consciously remove the negative emotions attached. I tell my mind and body to accept the challenge so it loses its power, and I force a smile on my face. I thank Jesus for the lesson I know I will soon learn. I ask Him to help me find a solution and infuse me with knowledge as I repeat my favorite words, "Jesus, I trust in You. Please help me, and show me what to do."

I pray, "Jesus, I want to have a grateful heart, not just in times of joy and peace, but especially in times of trouble and hardships. Thank You for helping me embrace this challenge. I love You."

12/16/09

Seek: I had the desire to not only hear God, but also to listen and follow Him into the depths of the unknown—all while having unwavering confidence that the unknown would bring me to my destiny.

Happy Anniversary, God! It was two years ago today that You showed me the magnitude of Your love, power, forgiveness, mercy, strength and unfathomable presence. It was my supernatural healing. The beginning of the restoration of my inner peace, the return of the true gifts and jewels in life that had been taken from me, the recognition of my tight grip in trying to control the outcome of my life, and my emphatic willingness to let go and finally let God.

For the whole of the day I consider this: He recognized my desire to not only hear Him, but also to listen and follow Him into the depths of the unknown. My confidence in Him was unwavering, and I had the wisdom to know that the unknown would bring me to my destiny. I often think back to December 16, 2007, the night I was touched by the Holy Spirit. Who would have thought the confirmation of this event was a simple red cardinal?

Today, the red cardinal is still my visual reminder of the power of God. It is amazing when I look back at where I was in my life at that time, reflect on the experience I have had and where I stand two years later. I thank Jesus, my life Coach, for His patience and love, for continually picking me up and brushing the dust off of me when I get knocked down, and for embracing me with His powerful Spirit and His strong words of encouragement. I am also grateful that I have the discipline, drive and determination that it requires of me to live in spirit with Christ. I realize, without a doubt, I can fall off of this course just as easily as I did before. I recognize that I need to *exercise God* in my life. My relationship with God requires time, thought and dedication —just as any other success in life requires. My greatest desire rests in training with God, and, in training with God, I am assured fulfillment and success.

As for today, I have just boarded a plane, and I am off to Deer Valley, Utah for a week of skiing. I am connecting with Stanton in the Houston airport, and I couldn't think of a better way to celebrate my spiritual awakening than with a man who is so true to my heart. Together, Stanton and I will ski the beautiful mountains that God created. We will glorify His work by enjoying His creation while we live, laugh, love and have fun!

12/17/10

Definition of wisdom is knowledge put to good use.

We arrived in Utah, and we were ready to ski. It's one of our favorite sports! As I approached the ski lodge storage facility, bundled up in my skiing gear, I politely requested my skis from an older gentleman working behind the counter, "Hi, I am here to pick up my skis. Here's my claim ticket." He looked at my name written on the tag, smiled and began to sing, "Kkkkkk-kkkkattttie, a beautiful ladddyyyy!" I smiled and laughed as I told the gentleman, "I have not heard that song in years. My grandfather use to sing that to me!" He continued smiling at me, but said nothing else. He slowly walked away to get my skis. In my heart, I knew Gramps was making his presence known to me—assuring me, once again, that he is smiling down on me as he watches over my journey.

12/18/09

Meditate: Sweet Jesus, together, hand in hand, we will thrive, and I will continue to keep my dreams alive.

As I am continually challenged by the fears that lie within me, I am slowly learning that thanking God actually makes me feel a little bit better. I read that when you thank God for problems, you are actually removing the fear from the problem and turning it into an experience from which you will learn and grow. I must admit that it is much easier said than done! I have to literally force my mind and thoughts to peacefully accept and embrace what is, rather than fighting them with my body's natural negative reaction. I remember, practice soon turns into habit.

The opportunity to practice thanking God came upon me the other night as I was lying in my bed. My fears crept into my mind, and it resulted in insomnia. Immediately, I began thanking God for this very moment, telling Him I want to learn and grow. I began to repeat the most comforting words that I know, "Jesus, I trust in You." As I slowly loosened the grip on my fears the most peaceful vision touched my soul—it was a beautiful, sunny day and although I was facing worries and fears, Jesus was with me to calmly and methodically walk me through them. We strolled along a beach, hand in hand, and we enjoyed the beauty of the day. The waves of my fears gently rolled across our feet, and they were swept away into the depths of the ocean. I suddenly felt the amazing peace, calm and security that Jesus brings to me.

Today I pray, "Sweet Jesus, together, hand in hand, we will thrive, and I will continue to keep my dreams alive."

12/24/09

I HAD TO TEAR YOU DOWN AND START ALL OVER. I
DUG DEEP BECAUSE YOUR FOUNDATION WAS NOT
STRONG ENOUGH TO BUILD UPON. I HAD TO GET YOU
READY BEFORE I COULD START CONSTRUCTION.

I am looking at my first blog entry. It reads, "Just as in a home
renovation, a soul renovation requires professional help (Thank
you, Jesus!), hard work (Practice! Practice! Practice!), dedication
(prayers and meditation), many tears (I cried myself a river, just
like Justin Timberlake) and THE WILL TO LET GO OF ALL
THAT ONCE STOOD AS A REPRESENTATION OF MYSELF
(Bye, bye, ego!). It also requires TRUST (for we walk by faith, not
by sight)."

12/25/09

Prayer: Sweet Jesus, this Christmas I wish to receive the gifts of wisdom, courage, strength and grace.

I was in church last night, and I was so thankful to be standing before God while reflecting on Jesus's journey with Mary and Joseph. I continue to ask God to infuse me with courage, wisdom, strength and grace. These are the gifts that I wish to receive on Christmas.

The homily began and soon my mind drifted away into my own thoughts, prayers and intentions. Jesus spoke to my heart, "Walk with Me! Walk with Me, Katie! Walk with Me! Trust in Me, Katie! Trust in Me! I AM with you. Do not worry about the future, for your fears may never come your way, and if they should, know that I will provide for you accordingly. Walk with Me!" The vision of us walking peacefully on the beach immediately sprang to my heart. I smiled, and I felt comfort knowing that as I face many challenges in life, I will remain at peace, walking with Jesus.

12/31/09

Lesson: God is fun!

It is hard to believe that another year has gone by so quickly. It feels as though it was yesterday when I was sitting at the kitchen table hearing Jesus encourage me by repeating, "Write. Write. Write."

Thankfully, I listened and I followed His direction—not knowing where it would lead me. Looking back, I can promise it has been by far the most healing, gratifying and rewarding time of my life. It has also been so much fun! I am surprised, and yet, not surprised when I randomly open up my journal, and my hand will land on an entry that needs to touch my heart again. It takes me back to that very real moment where a lesson was taught to me. The luxury of rereading the entry is reinforcement I get from the lesson learned. Another blessing! I look back on this past year, and it is full of so many beautiful events. While also riddled with difficult challenges, the memories of the challenges fade away. It is the moments of victory, love and peace that stand present in my heart.

I reflect on my journey with Jesus, and I can't help but to send out a 100-watt smile! I laugh in delight of the sweet and funny moments we have shared together, and I feel beautiful inside. I see myself stretching, standing in the sun and anticipating every run. I hear "our" songs and get an extra beat in my step. On my weakest and most fatigued days, I meditate on the dreams, messages and words spoken to me, and my courage and perseverance are restored. I thank Jesus, Mary, Joseph and my team of Heavenly Hosts for their love and support. I know that I would not be where I am today if I had not surrendered and invited God into my life.

I know I have a multitude of lessons to grasp and that learning is never ending. I embrace that fact and I know, in the end, it will form me into the person that I am meant to be. If I could offer any advice, it would be that in order to have a healthy relationship with God it has to *be real*. It must be real in the way that when you interact with God, it should be just as personal as it is when you are with a best friend, spouse, partner or companion. You must nurture the relationship, respect each other, love, talk, listen and take action on directions. Most importantly, have fun!

1/1/10

Challenge: Discover and fulfill your unique role in life.

As I enter a new year—my goal is to continue living in peace. I pray for my mind and heart to always be at rest, replacing every anxious and fearful thought with love and trust. I pray for continued growth in discovering and fulfilling my unique role in life.

Jesus, I am thrilled to walk, IN + LOVE, with You.

1/7/10

Challenge: Take the TIME to set your heart on God, everyday at
          3:00 p.m.

I have been in Houston this past week. I was in the Decorative
Center returning carpet samples when I walked in the Stark
showroom. I saw a beautiful woman sitting behind the front desk,
and I could sense that she was a peaceful soul as she politely
greeted me in a warm, Southern manner. She called a salesman
over to assist me, and Anne-Marie came my way with a warm and
friendly smile. We stood at the desk to greet each other, in an
effort to discuss my interior design project, but before I knew it all
three of us were wrapped up in a conversation that had nothing to
do with my order and everything to do with God. The receptionist
mentioned a daily devotional that she recently read: praying to
overcome the fear of loving again. We all began singing our
praises to God and professing our love and faith when my 3:00
p.m. prayer alarm sounded on my phone. I smiled and showed
them my phone, which displayed, "Pray" when the clock strikes
three. I laughed as I spoke, "What perfect timing God always has
in revealing Himself!" As our laughter settled down, both women
told me how they loved the idea of setting their phone alarm to a
3:00 p.m. prayer time. After wrapping up my business, I left the
showroom full of joy in knowing I brought two more people to
God, every day at 3:00 p.m.!

1/8/10

WALK WITH ME TODAY, IN CONFIDENCE.

As I sit down this morning to meditate and pray, I ask Jesus to speak to my heart, "Jesus, please tell me what I need to hear." I sit and wait patiently for His response while I continue to pray. After some time had passed, out of nowhere, I heard, "Eradicate your fears." Hmmmm, I reflect on the word "eradicate." I know that it is a strong word, and my curiosity wants to know exactly what He means. I pick up my iPhone and Google "eradicate." The definition, "To pull up by the roots, 2. To do away with as completely as if pulling up by the roots," I think to myself, "That is the perfect verb for Him to use. That is so Jesus!" If there is one lesson He continues to drill into my heart it is to never take a shortcut, and quick fixes never withstand the test of time. If I only wipe my fears away at the surface, the "root" will remain, and eventually the fears will grow back.

The word, ERADICATE, is also a verb. This is when I hear, "Action!" I must apply this action into my daily life. I can easily sit at this table and write and feel—with conviction—the Holy Spirit is upon me. I trust Jesus, but I doubt my own ability at times. I think, "What if I am somehow hearing Him wrong?" The doubt halts progression. I ask Jesus with disappointment, "Why does this happen to me?" He responds, "You are still seeking approval and validation from others. Seek approval and validation from Me and ME ALONE. Whom do you choose to follow?"

Once again, Jesus is right. I worry too much about what others will think. I need to follow what I believe. I must pull up, from the roots, ALL of my fears. I remind myself that Jesus is the ultimate gardener—He wants to heal, but the process can't begin until the root of the problem is completely removed. Otherwise, the weed will slowly grow back in time.

I hear Jesus speak to me firmly as I am closing my journal, "Walk with Me today, *in confidence*!"

1/9/10

Meditate: Timing. Purpose. Trust in God.

I returned to the Stark showroom on January 6th to pick up samples for another client. I was delighted to see Ann Marie again, and we told each other how thrilled we were to have met. During our conversation she told me that she has a beautiful marriage—she explained how every year their love only grows stronger. She said she felt God's hand in their relationship, and she believes this is why they are strong as a couple. My soul literally began to dance as she said so peacefully, "Our challenges and burdens only feel half of their weight, and our joy and happiness is doubled because we have each other." That is a true partnership. That is a real marriage. That is what I want!

Curiously, I asked Anne Marie, " How did you know he was the one?" She responded without hesitation, "Character. His character told me everything I needed to know." I mentioned that I was divorced and how frightening it has been for me to love again. I told her about Stanton, the story of how we met, how I had been hospitalized and that Stanton never left my side. She looked me in my eyes intently and said, "I believe God wanted to show you Stanton's character. He wanted you to see who he really is." My eyes filled with tears, Ann Marie's comment provided me with further validation and more reason to trust.

On this very day, my best friend, Nicole, forwarded an e-mail to me. Although the e-mail was sent to her on September 20, 2009, she forgot to forward it to me, until today. The e-mail was from Joanna Nelson. She was discussing my hospitalization. Joanna told Nicole's mother, Roslyn, about the amazing sense of urgency she felt from her deceased daughter, Jo Beth, to contact me. I ask myself, *What are the chances that I would talk about my hospitalization to Anne Marie, that she would in turn share her thoughts with me, and that I would receive the forgotten e-mail— all on the very same day?* There are no coincidences. I believe timing. I believe purpose. I believe, once again, this is my confirmation from God and my Heavenly Hosts that my illness did serve a purpose. It was an opportunity for me to learn, and to trust in God—it was an opportunity to see, feel and experience Stanton's character, loyalty.

1/18/10

Challenge: The cycle of life, this is what I must learn to embrace, the beginning, the middle...and the end.

I picked up one of my favorite books yesterday, *Lead like Jesus*, by Ken Blanchard and Phil Hodges. As I flipped through the pages, I paused when my highlight caught my eye. It is an important paragraph, a message I must master. The authors compare life, people, relationships, possessions and careers as being "leased." They explain that God only "leases" these luxuries to us and that any of them, or all of them, can be taken away from us at any time, upon His discretion. In life, everything has a beginning, middle and an end. It is simply the cycle of life.

Today, I will continue to practice, loosening my grip by reminding myself to enjoy and appreciate what I do have today, for I never know when the lease will expire. The cycle of life—this is what I must learn to embrace, the beginning, the middle...*and the end*.

1/19/10

THE TIMING IS RIGHT.

Last night, I curled up in bed, closed my eyes and I began to pray to God, "Dear God, please confirm that I am on Your path. I know what my heart desires, but I want to be certain that I am in sync with Your plans and Your time schedule, not mine. Should I be walking too fast, moving too slow or moving in the wrong direction, I will expect you to bring me to a halt, for something to arise that will change my course. If it does, I will know it is from You, but if it does not, I will know all is well, and I will continue to move forward. Sweet Jesus, please keep Your loving and protecting arms around me and my family. I love You so much, and I am so grateful for all that You do. Goodnight." I soon fell asleep.

That night, in my dream, Jesus was encouraging me to stay on the path I am on. He assured me I am exactly where I am meant to be. I spoke out loud, "I understand. Okay. I will." I also remember Him repeating over and over again, "The timing is right." In my dream, Stanton was sitting on a sofa with me—his arm was around me, and his smile is genuine—I recall a young lady approaching us with a smile, she looked at Stanton and said, "Everyone has embraced you. We are waiting." Stanton simply continued to smile.

I have an amazing amount of peace this morning. I feel such relief and joy in knowing that I am exactly where I am suppose to be in our journey. I FEEL IT.

Houston it is!

1/20/10

Thanksgiving: I am grateful for having the courage to believe in God.

Yesterday, Kim, a dear friend of mine from Houston mailed me a note. She always sends the most beautiful words of wisdom, so I anxiously opened the letter. I pulled out the paper, unfolded it, and there it was—a magazine article with a big, bright red cardinal at the top. I began smiling, although I had not even read the content. I felt joy in knowing that when I shared my red cardinal story with her, it touched her heart, and as a result, she became more aware of their presence.

The article is titled, "On the Wing's of Love," "Heaven often sends cardinals as a comforting message of love, as *Woman's World* reader Sherry Sheffer of New Bloomfield, Pennsylvania discovered..."

After reading the article, I realized it was my confirmation that not only can a red cardinal be a heavenly reminder, but confirmation that dreams can carry messages. Sherry, the woman in the article, had a deceased brother who came to her in a dream. He told her that when she saw a red cardinal, it would serve as a reminder that he is with her.

Yesterday, I wrote about my dream. Today, I received an article about a significant dream and the symbolism of a red cardinal. There are *no coincidences*. The timing is precise—just as God would have it. I am grateful for having the courage to believe. It would certainly be easier for me to dismiss everything that happens in life as coincidence. But, knowing, feeling and believing in God's work far out weighs my ego. Sherry Sheffer, thank you for sharing your beautiful story. God, thank You for making sure her article landed safely in my hands.

1/26/10

Challenge: Trust the "pass" that God throws your way.

How about the Saints? Yes, the New Orleans Saints are headed to the Super Bowl for the very first time in history! The city is on fire, and I feel so blessed to be witnessing a defeated team turn into a winning team. The Saints represent PERSEVERANCE, ENDURANCE, MANAGEMENT, MOBILITY, BALANCE, TRUST, FAITH AND BELIEF!

I can't help but recognize the amount of TRUST that Drew Brees has in his teammates. Every time he throws a pass, he must TRUST that a teammate will be exactly where he's supposed to be in order to complete the play. It made me realize the extraordinary amount of planning, coordinating and execution of both coaches and players. It requires listening to directions, taking action when directions are given and trusting that each player will do his part to the best of their ability. It means that if the opposing team interferes with the execution, you are not to waste time focusing on what could have been done to change the past play. Instead, move forward and focus on what needs to be done to successfully execute the next play.

I think football is a great parallel to life and our relationship with God. These very elements are present everyday—if we work as a team, dedicate ourselves to believing and having faith in winning, if we commit ourselves to following God's direction, if we take action when direction is given, if we trust God enough to recognize that the pass He throws to us has a purpose. If the pass is intercepted, we are to continue to move forward and fight for the next opportunity. As you gain confidence in God (just as teammates gain confidence in the quarterback), you can overcome the challenges in life and reach victory.

As easy and beautiful as it sounds, you can't just show up on the field for game day. Just as with God, life requires daily practice and hard work. It involves both joy and pain. Winning does not happen overnight. It has taken the Saints forty-three years to get to the Super Bowl, and the fight is not over, but the victory has already been accomplished in my eyes—the victory is celebrated in the fact that the Saints never gave up, despite being called "The worst team in the NFL." They did not listen to the opinions of others—rather they believed the truth in their hearts, the truth that they could overcome adversity and become a winning team.

Nothing is impossible. Dreams are realized.

1/30/10

Meditate: I will detach myself from other people's opinion.

Yesterday was Sacred Heart's annual mass, "Let your Light Shine." Stanton came to New Orleans, and Susan and Sophia asked him to join us. He was delighted to be included, and he joyfully accepted the invitation.

When you are divorced with children, you face the challenge of bringing someone new into your life. Not only do you have to think about your own needs and desires, but those of your children as well. I reminded myself from the very beginning that my girls would learn from my actions more than by my verbal lessons. I also knew that not only are my actions important, but learning from my *interactions* was equally as powerful. I soon realized how fortunate I am—fortunate in that my daughters could witness the love and happiness between us. I am fortunate my daughters love me so much, and that my love and happiness brings them great love and happiness. I am fortunate that Stanton's positive energy and love for life infected all of us. We are blessed because Stanton is respectful of his position in our family, and he is in no way trying to compete or take the place of the girl's father. He genuinely wants to be a trustworthy, reliable male figure and an added support for the girls.

Having that said, I feel guilty at times for being happy and enjoying my life. When I am out with Stanton, and we run into family or friends of my former husband, my joy turns to a wave of anxiety and guilt. I clam up, keep my distance, and hide my smile and laughter in front of them—I think I am somehow being disrespectful for finding happiness and moving forward.

I experienced this anxious feeling yesterday. As Stanton, Susan, Sophia and myself drove to the Sacred Heart mass we sang and danced to the songs on the radio—we were all laughing and having fun. We parked the car and headed into the Nims Center, where the mass was being held. As we made our way to our seats, from out of the blue, Sophia started to withdraw. Not only could I see it, but I felt it. I imagined all eyes watching us, the little broken family with their mom's boyfriend. I felt tension, nerves and discomfort. I continued to remind myself to let it go, but as I watched Sophia squirm, pull away from Stanton and clinch onto my arm, it only intensified what I was already feeling. Stanton politely tried to engage Sophia in conversation, but as he did, she frowned and scooted even closer to me and buried her head in my side. I thought to myself, *Great! Now it looks like Sophia doesn't like Stanton. This makes me look like a terrible mother—me putting my children in this awkward situation.*

In my mind, I could only *imagine* what everyone in the auditorium was saying about us. To add to the equation, my former mother-in-law appeared and sat with us. Don't get me wrong, I am very thankful she was there to show the girls her love and support, and I welcome and appreciate it more than she will ever realize. My fear was not that she was with us, but that she was witnessing Stanton interacting with the girls for the very first time. She was witnessing us at our most vulnerable moment, in public and uncomfortable in our new roles. Her eyes and expression spoke volumes—I could only imagine her thoughts and the sadness at seeing her grandchildren with me and another man. I just wanted to leave so I could relieve the lump that was forming in my throat. Guilt and shame for being happy were breaking me down...and Sophia. Susan and Stanton were the only ones at ease—smiling and relaxing in their chairs. I wanted to feel like them! I wanted my negative emotions to disappear. I immediately prayed to Jesus asking for His help, but absolutely nothing changed. I continued to battle my feelings by repeating, "Jesus, I trust in You. Jesus, I trust in You." I missed every word the priest said because I was too overwhelmed and wrapped up in a war with myself. Frustrated and embarrassed, I asked Jesus, "What are You trying to teach me?" I still heard no response. Finally, after struggling for quite some time, I remembered where to find my ammunition—I began to focus on the truth. The truth is that the girls and I love Stanton. The truth is we all have fun together. The truth is we are *all* excited when we are together. The truth is Stanton takes his time to play and interact with the girls just as a friend and supporter should. The truth is that Stanton very much loves *all* of us. I thought to myself, *If only everyone here knew the truth. The truth is that this moment is not an accurate representation of the positive energy we all have together.*

I remembered another important lesson Jesus has been trying to teach me, "Detach yourself from other people's opinion." I finally realized I was trying to put on a show for people. I was more consumed with what image I was projecting rather than resting in the truth. In that moment, I was living for others and not myself. I know this situation was presented to me as an opportunity to "eradicate my fears." I believe this situation was an opportunity to face my fears, knowing that in facing them, I will soon be free of them.

2/8/10

Challenge: Never tire, never give up and always FINISH
STRONG!

The Saints won the Super Bowl last night! It is a dream that came true for an entire city. Never give up and always, FINISH STRONG!

2/12/10

YES, I LOVE YOU! YES, I AM WITH YOU! YES, IT IS ME, JESUS!

I was typing out my journal last night when out from nowhere I heard internally, "It is time to get more P.R. Get your work published." I knew that the thought was not my own and that Jesus was giving me direction. I paused to reflect on what I heard, and I could literally feel the power of Spirit. The feeling is very distinct, and it differs from any other feeling I have ever felt before. The feeling speaks to me, "Yes, I love you! Yes, I am with you! Yes, it is Me, Jesus! Yes, I planted that thought. Listen to my direction. Take action." I acknowledge what has just been spoken to me by telling Jesus, through my heart, that I understand Him, and I will follow His direction. I leaned over to my desk drawer, and I took out a sticky note—I wrote, "Photograph Lisa's home. Send pictures to Tria." Shortly afterwards, on the very same night, my client/friend that I just made reference to called me. I told Lisa I had just written myself a note to photograph her house on my next trip to Houston. I asked her for permission, and I explained to her that I would like to try to get her home published. She agreed, and I set up the date and time.

The next morning, I had an e-mail sitting in my inbox. It was from Tria, the photographer from New York, the one I had just made note to contact! We hadn't communicated in months. Her e-mail told me she had shown my work to an agency specializing in U.K. publications—she wanted to know whether I would be interested in pursuing that avenue. She also asked me if I could take some photographs of the home in Houston that I had been designing as she would like to scout the home for publication!

Once again, notice the *perfect timing* of the sequence of events and the players involved. There are *no coincidences*. I am delighted simply knowing I received a message and directions from Jesus. I listened, I understood, I made a notation, and He guided the appropriate players my way...just like that! I love when I catch His pass! Now, it is *my job* to follow through and take action.

I am scheduled to photograph the house next Friday at 9:00 a.m. I will e-mail the photographs directly to Tria. I know that what happens next will be just right—when He thinks the timing is right!

2/14/10

Question: How do you recognize TRUE love?

When I think about the most genuine form of true love, one name comes to my heart, Jesus. He is the ultimate example of love.

"Jesus, I remember praying to You after my divorce. I told You I did not know how to recognize true love. I told You how frightened I was to love again. I recall You whispering words of wisdom, 'The love and the feelings you have for Me are genuine and true. Use them as a guide. Focus on the feelings and emotions I bring to you.'"

With that said, I closed my eyes and I reflected only on Jesus and the feelings that I feel when His Spirit is with me. I begin to write. I feel a fullness in my heart and spirit, a feeling of being lifted, peace, warmth, a stirring of emotions deep in my soul, smiles, laughter, comfort, joy, protection, unconditional love, complete selflessness, respect, loyalty and trust. The emotions are all mixed together, and it is so amazingly strong that I feel explosive!

Jesus speaks to my heart, "Not only do I give these feelings to you, but you also give these feelings to Me. Both of us, giving and receiving." I knew my love for Jesus, and the love He has for me is the most genuine and healthy form of love I could ever experience. My goal was to find similar qualities in my life partner.

I am pleased to report that the mission has been accomplished. Jesus and Mary, thank you for always helping me!

2/20/10

Straight from my heart: I love You, God!

Yesterday, Stanton told me he would be taking me somewhere special for the weekend. He said I needed to finish work by 11:00 a.m. and to pack an overnight bag. He would not tell me our destination, only that I would need a pair of boots for the day and a dress for dinner. I must admit, I felt butterflies swirling around in my belly, and I thought, "Could this be it?" Stanton and I talk about getting married often, but I want to be surprised. My only thought was, *time*. Regardless of the outcome, I knew I was going away with Stanton on a romantic adventure, and I knew we would have an amazing time, as always.

After I photographed my client's house, Stanton picked me up and we headed out of town. The only information I could gather was that we were headed north, driving down highway 290. I loved the fact I had absolutely no idea where we were going.

An hour into our drive, Stanton began to veer off to the right of the highway and we took the exit to Washington, Texas. I was thrilled to see we were headed into the Hill Country because it is so beautiful! I love the simplicity of a little small town and the green rolling hills. I love watching the animals graze the land and feeling the peacefulness that fills the air. As I am taking all of these precious moments in, we wind down the road and approach a large ranch. The manicured and pristine property was guarded by two large stonewalls and a security gate with a call box at the entry. I knew we were entering exclusive grounds that could hardly be described as a "ranch." The sign read, "The Inn at Dos Brisas." Stanton rolled down his window, pressed the call button and announced our arrival—the gates slowly opened up for us. I sat up straighter in my seat, took in a deep breath, exhaled and looked around. The grounds were absolutely gorgeous! I was so thrilled feeling, pure joy, pure love and total relaxation.

We slowly pulled up to the main house and we were greeted by a row of staff members. As Stanton put the car in park, they opened our doors, greeted us with warm, friendly smiles and said, "Hello, Mr. Scott. Welcome! We will be taking your car to your casita, and we will unpack it for you. Please step into this golf cart and we will bring you to the horse stables where someone will be waiting for you." I thought, "Horseback riding? I have not been horseback riding in years!" I felt like I was a young girl back at Big Tree Day Camp in New Orleans, Louisiana, and I was excited! As we entered the stables we we're greeted by our guide. She introduced me to, Mambo, the horse I would be riding. She described him as calm, old, wise and the leader of the pack. I was delighted, and I climbed up on Mambo and sat comfortably on this beautiful creature. Stanton mounted his horse as well and off we went. After touring the property, we stopped along a creek where a picnic table had been set with a beautiful picnic basket. The chef had prepared a gourmet lunch, wine and water. As we ate, we gazed into each other's eyes, kissed sweetly and admired our surroundings. It was awesome! Afterwards, we slowly made our way back to the stable, where Stanton told me he had a special dessert planned. He stipulated that before dessert we would need to go by the casita. As we walked into the door of The Magnolia, the name of our casita, Stanton said, "Katie, I hear your prayer alarm going off." Picking up my iPhone, I thought to myself, *It's 3:00 p.m., a special time for prayer, and I believe something special is about to happen. This is God's blessing.* I slid the alarm off and in my heart I said, "I love you, God." Stanton grabbed his backpack and told me to follow him. We climbed into our golf cart, and he took me to a heart-shaped pond at the front of the property. It was chilly that day so he laid blankets out for us. He covered me up to keep me warm as he pulled out his backpack and said, "Katie, these past ten months have been so amazing, and I truly love you with all of my heart." He then pulled out his portable iPod speakers and said, "I made a play list of all of the songs that remind me of you, our songs." He pressed play, reached for a bottle of champagne, poured two glasses and said, "For dessert, I brought ten of your favorite things—each one representing a month we have been together." I laughed as he handed me a Hershey bar, Cracker Jacks, Doritos, Starbursts, a Diet Coke and all of my little guilty pleasures in life. My laughter soon turned into a sudden wave of tears—I was overcome with emotions as I heard Coldplay sing, "Miss You." My tears represented both joy and victory. I realized what beauty and great love I would have missed out on if I had allowed my fear to control me. In the beginning of our courtship it was this very song that made me realize that I can't be afraid, and Stanton was not someone to pass by. I received the warning sign when I began to miss him tremendously, simply thinking about him not being a part of my life. In my heart, I thanked God profusely. Stanton comforted me, and he also became emotional—we feel each other's love.

Just as I began to dry my tears, "Let It Be" started to play and before I knew it Stanton was down on one knee telling me how much he loved me and how he wants us to spend the rest of our lives together. He slowly reached into his pocket and opened up a small box that held three precious ring bands. He asked, "Will you marry me?" At this point, we were both crying again. I jumped up out of the chair, wrapped my arms around him and exclaimed, "Yes! I love you so much!" We held each other as tight as possible, and Stanton lifted me up so high that my feet no longer touched the ground. Stanton then pulled out four pennies from his pocket, "These pennies are for us to wish upon. I want you to walk with me to the edge of the pond. It will be our wishing well." We made our way to the water's edge and faced each other. He continued, "The first two pennies date back to our birth years, 1971 and 1968. I want both of us to close our eyes and make a personal wish—this is for something that we want for ourselves, not for each other." We closed our eyes, made a wish and threw the pennies in the pond. He then held up the third penny, "This penny is from 2009. It represents the year we met each other. It symbolizes our appreciation for God, for our meeting and for all of the love He brought to us. I want us to hold hands and say a prayer of thanksgiving and throw the penny in the pond, together." Stanton had one penny left. He said, "This penny is from 2010. It is a representation of today and our future, us moving forward together." We held hands again, said a prayer of hope for our future to be full of love, health and happiness, and we threw the penny in our wishing well. We embraced each other and continued to cry tears of love and joy. I praised Stanton for his thoughtfulness and for all of the details of this amazing day. I could not have felt any more loved! We toasted our champagne glasses, we laughed, kissed and embraced this beautiful memory.

The day after our engagement, I had to drive back to New Orleans. As I drove down I-10 it dawned on me that "Pennies are from heaven." I smiled, thinking about the Chris Botti CD, *To Love Again*, that I play daily as I work, and listen to the rendition of "Pennies from Heaven." Once again, I shake my head in disbelief and I think to myself, *there are no coincidences. Once again, thank You, God!*

2/24/10

Meditate: A garden in full bloom is the best representation of my love and unity with God.

Stanton and I have set a date. It looks as if I will be a June bride! June has always been one of my favorite months of the year. I hear the word "June" and automatically think about my birthday, the smell of freshly cut grass, a bright sun shining, pools sparkling, laughter of children, the smell of sunscreen, tank tops, shorts, flip-flops, beaches and many barbeques. Now, I get to add one more very special event to that list, our wedding!

We have decided to get married at The Inn at Dos Brisas. I want our surroundings to reflect who we are as a couple. Nature is so close to my heart, and all I could envision was Stanton and I standing in a garden that was in full bloom—a garden in bloom is the best representation of what my love and unity with God resembles.

When Stanton and I pulled into Dos Brisas he specifically pointed out the rose garden—it had just been pruned so it was very bare, but I had the vision to see past the present condition, and I smiled at all of the beauty to come. I literally felt a wave of excitement when I saw the arched rose trellis. It immediately brought my heart back to a dream that I had on February 25, 2008, *prior to meeting Stanton*. In my dream it was my wedding, and I was standing under an arched trellis! An older gentleman walked up to me and placed his arm through mine so we were locked together. Although I did not recognize Him, I understood Him to be my Heavenly Father. He asked, "Are you ready?" I responded, "Is he nervous?" While taking a step forward, He said, "Well, let's go see." As we walked together, I said to myself as I looked around, "I didn't want a big, fancy wedding." From up above I heard the voice of a sweet, young, female angel innocently saying, "...but I thought she always wanted a Cinderella wedding..." I remember thinking, in my dream, *what is going on?* As we head towards a long line of groomsmen standing in single file line, we begin to approach whom I believe to be the groom, and we stop next to him as he continues to look forward. My Father asks, "Are you nervous?" and the gentleman responds, while still looking straight ahead, "Not really." I ask the groomsmen, "You really didn't want all of this, did you?" and he bluntly responds, "No." In an instant, I am literally swept away onto the dance floor by another groomsman. This groomsman is a very tall, young man dressed in a tuxedo. I can't see his face, but I can see the depth in his eyes. In return, I can see him looking into my eyes—his gaze is so distinct and intense that through his eyes, I see my own eyes, and they are lined with a sultry, soft, peacock green and dark brown eye shadow, and my lashes are laced with a light coat of mascara. I can literally feel his amazingly strong love for me, and the magnitude is so great that it's almost hard for me to believe. I can feel his thoughts: he feels I am the most beautiful woman he's ever seen. In return, I can feel my amazingly strong love and admiration for him. We are completely connected on all levels and just as you would see in a science fiction movie, we are suddenly meshed into one as we slowly spin beyond the earth. I can see the darkness of space as we rise into eternity, but we were glowing with light and the stars surround us. Suddenly, we zoom back to the present, and we are back out on the dance floor, where we slowly begin to kiss; it is the most passionate, beautiful and real kiss I've ever experienced. It's so strong that, once again, I can literally feel it. As he stands, his height towers over me, and his eyes never leave mine as he bends down on one knee and hums a tune, "Na, na, na, na, na, na, na..." I wake up.

The dream was so unbelievably realistic that I sat up quickly in my bed, and I had to question myself several times—was it a dream or did it really happen? Confused, I ask, out loud, "God, what was that about? Who was that tall man? I thought I would end up with someone else I had in mind?" I lay back down in my bed for a long time, reviewing every single little detail. I spoke out loud, "God, that was the strongest love I have ever felt. He really loved me, and I really loved him. That is the kind of love that I have always dreamed of having. My God, that felt so real. I want that!" The feelings and details were so specific and electrifying that I shared the story with my mother that same morning. I knew the dream was revealing something to me as I felt it from the greatest depths of my soul. I repeatedly questioned my mom for the next several days by asking, "Who was that tall guy?"

The following day, my curiosity drove me to Barnes & Noble so I could research dream interpretations. Once I found the book, I decided to focus on the meaning of eyes because in the dream they had the greatest power and detail. It stated that when eyes are looking into one another, it's symbolic of two soul mates searching for each other!

Yes, Stanton is 6'4". Yes, his eyes have always spoken to me, and they were strangely familiar to me ever since the day we met. Yes, our love for each other is electrifying. Yes, I often find the magnitude of our love almost hard to believe. I know, beyond a doubt, Stanton was the tall man that was revealed to me in my dream. Stanton is my soul mate.

My heart leaps to the words spoken by the priest at St. Patrick's church, "There are *no coincidences*!"

2/26/10

CONTINUE TO GROW.

As I sit and meditate on my favorite pictures of both Jesus and Mary, I suddenly become overwhelmed with gratitude. I thank them for such amazing inspiration and for helping me in such a beautiful way. I feel the rush of the Holy Spirit smother me in love, and I feel the stirring of my emotions from deep within. It is unstoppable.

I asked Jesus to allow me to be an instrument of His love. I speak to Him, "Jesus, I am scared. I have never felt anything so strong and powerful. I hear you tell me to speak but I cringe at the thought of speaking in public. Yet, I want to do whatever You need me to do—I want to help God. I would not be where I am today without Your help and guidance. I want to return the gift by giving God something significant and meaningful. Please guide me."

My heart went back to a quote I once read. It stated that whenever you are comfortable, it is time to get uncomfortable for this is how we learn and grow.

I hear Jesus speak to my heart, "Continue to grow."

3/9/10

"Ode to Sweet Jesus"

Katie: Jesus, Jesus, Sweet Jesus! Why is it people see You from afar? It is right here, right now, where You really are. I see no need for such formality, although, I mean no disrespect, rather simplicity, and awe, and love, and respect. I pray for others to see You as I do: a friend to have, to hold and someone to talk too. Why must the mind be so confining and the eyes of sight so defying? Open your heart, it's You I see, You, standing here, right in front of me! To have, to hold, to love, to protect, my Sweet Jesus, for You, I have total love and respect.

Jesus: Intimacy here is what needs to be seen: Me loving you, you loving Me

Katie: Caught up in laughter, brings tears to my face. A run, a walk, a big, warm embrace! Errands with You lighten my mood, having a driver chauffer all of my moves! Dancing, why not? Who doesn't like to have fun? The beat of your heart is my rhythm and my tune. Songs on the radio, You serenade me and I serenade You. Oh, once again, the tears come rolling in. I feel You with me. I want to start again.

3/23/10

Meditate: St. Christopher, protect me.

Stanton and I went to Washington, D.C. this past weekend to join in a wedding celebration. We had an amazing time visiting with Stanton's family and walking the streets. My favorite stopping point was the Basilica of The Immaculate Conception. Stanton, knowing how I adore Mary, was so thoughtful in making sure I visited this amazing church. I cherished him being there with me. The church was insanely gorgeous! The mosaics and the details were endless. I could not stop thinking about the amount of work that went into designing and creating the magnitude of beauty that stood before us. It was almost overwhelming.

My favorite shrine represented The Miraculous Medal of Mary. It is sacred to me because I see it as a symbol of her strength, courage and her vision. We took time to light candles for our families. We knelt down in thanksgiving before Mary's powerful shrine. I asked her to please bless us on our journey. In my heart, I knew her intercession would be required and her example was to be followed.

Before leaving the Basilica, I asked Stanton if we could browse through the gift shop. I love spiritual books, jewelry and accessories. Stanton and I were on opposite ends of the store when I heard him shout across the way, "Katie, come over here and look at all of these medals. Maybe, I should get one?" I didn't want his desire to be fleeting, so I quickly walked over to him. He stood before a multitude of Saints. I knew I had to optimize the situation so I told him I wanted to buy one for him just as he had bought one for me last year on my birthday. He then asked, "Which one should I get?" As we spun the carousel around, St. Christopher sparkled in my eye. I smiled and I said to Stanton, "This is it. St. Christopher.

He is the saint who offers protection while traveling." He replied, "Great! St. Christopher it is! My dad gave me one of these when I was little." We had the clerk open up the locked case, and he pulled out St. Christopher.

After I purchased the medal for Stanton, we decided to go back into the church so we could bless it and somehow make it even more special. Not knowing what I was doing, I decided to take the medal out of the box and submerge it in the holy water that was by the front entrance of the church. I made the sign of the cross, and I genuflected towards the main alter. Stanton, even more clueless than I was, followed my lead. I whispered to him, "Let's go back to my favorite shrine, The Miraculous Medal of Mary. We can ask her to bless the medal." Hand in hand, Stanton and I approached Mary's shrine, knelt down in the pew, and I quietly asked, "Mary, please watch over Stanton and protect his soul. We are both making a pledge to you. We want to do all we can to fulfill our purpose in life and to live God's will. Please assist us in all we are asked to do." Stanton stepped in and he spoke as well. I am always surprised to hear how eloquently he prays and I can't help but to wonder at times, *where is this coming from? It is so beautiful!* I couldn't help but to smile and giggle from within, as I seriously thought, "Jesus, what are You up to?"

April 5, 2010

Meditate: Welcome the Holy Spirit to soar into your soul.

This past week I felt an unusual hunger for Jesus and I wanted Him to feel my love. I reached over to my bedside table to pick up the *Handbook of Devotion to Divine Mercy*. I clasped it in my hand as if it was His hand, and I held it tightly as I slept through the night, all while whispering thoughts of love and appreciation to Him. A day later, I realized it was Holy Week. I recognized the *perfect timing* of the significant feelings I was instinctively feeling.

I thank Mary for being so courageous during His passion. I express tremendous gratitude; feelings of appreciation immediately fill me up to confirm the presence of His loving Spirit. In this moment, I recognize it's a feeling that is simply undeniable. A feeling that sets me free. A feeling that reminds me, "I AM with you." A feeling that speaks volumes and boldly professes, "I love you!"

4/8/10

Perspective: Associate spirituality with adventure.

Yesterday, I went to Scriptura in New Orleans, to pick up our wedding invitations. I approached the front desk and a nice gentleman greeted me, "May I help you?" I responded, "Yes, I am here to pick up an order for Katie Stassi and Stanton Scott." Before I could even politely smile, he was already handing me a copy of our invitation. I was ecstatic when I saw the clean, simple, elegant and cheerful design, which is exactly what I envisioned for us. I smiled as I read, "katie and stanton" centered on the card and written in a perfect yellow pantone and set in a free style font in lowercase print. I continued to read, "Together with their families, Katherine Ridgeway Stassi and Stanton Howard Scott, request the pleasure of your company at their marriage, Saturday, the fifth of June, two thousand ten, at four o'clock in the afternoon, The Inn at Dos Brisas, Washington, Texas, Reception to Follow." The wedding was officially in writing, and I felt genuine happiness and excitement.

As I was checking out at the counter, I began to have a conversation with the gentleman who was helping me. He mentioned his other store location, and for some reason, I asked, "Do you work with your wife?" he responded, "Yes. We are not together every day, but we do work together." Instinctively, I knew exactly who his wife was—she helped me and Stanton when we were selecting and designing our invitations. For whatever reason, I felt a glimmer of inspiration and excitement as my thoughts quickly turned towards the possibility of Stanton and I working together as a team, in some capacity, in the future. At that very moment, Margaret, his wife, swept up to the front desk looking just as beautiful and peaceful as she did when we first met. She exclaimed, "Your invitation turned out beautiful!" I responded, "Thank you so much for all of your help. I absolutely love it. They're perfect!" She smiled. "I just want you to know that I can see that Stanton just wants to take care of you, and he wants to be with you for everything. You walk together very easily, and you actually remind me of David and me." I joyfully smiled at what she was sharing me. I told her Stanton is a blessing to me, and I give thanks to God because He arranged our meeting. Margaret quickly and casually interjected, "Yes. Me too! The same thing happened. I said a novena and within one week I met David! Before we knew it, we were engaged and married. We continue to renew our vows wherever we go because we just love getting married! David is a convert, and we often travel with our priest. We all love to travel together, and he marries us wherever we are!" I laughed. I was genuinely thrilled for their joyful marriage. She chimed in, "Just because we are converts doesn't mean we don't like to have fun, and I can promise you David is one of the coolest guys I know." I knew exactly what she meant. I smile at the truth and think to myself, "Living through God is the ultimate adventure of a lifetime. I'm told God lives through each of us, if we allow Him. That being the case, I am going to make sure that *we* have a good time!"

4/9/10

Meditate: Destiny.

One year ago, I met destiny—happy anniversary, Stanton! Cheers, to love and divine intervention!

Thank you, Jesus, Mary and my team of Heavenly Hosts! Amen!

4/11/10

Inspiration: What a difference a year can make.

As Stanton and I placed our wedding invitations into the envelopes, Stanton turned to me, "Who would have thought when we met one year ago that this is what we would be doing today? Here I am, sitting with you, stuffing envelopes—for our wedding! Whew! What a difference a year makes!" We both laughed and we leaned into each other to kiss on that happy note. I responded playfully, "Thank God!" and together we sealed our fate.

4/28/10

Practice: Total dependence on God and God alone.

Yesterday, I belly crawled under my bed to retrieve moving boxes. I realized how fast these two years have flown by, and my move to New Orleans seems like yesterday.

After Stanton and I get married in June, the girls and I will be moving back to Houston, so I started to pack a few of my belongings that had been stored in a closet. One by one, the reminders of my past began to stir inside of me. Soon enough, a lump formed inside of my throat and tears began to fall. I was crying not because I missed what once was, but because a marriage failed, and a family was torn apart. I sat down on the floor and I closed my eyes. I prayed to God, asking Him for love, peace and happiness for *all* of us.

Shortly thereafter, I came across a stack of pictures—photographs of me and Stanton. I studied them, one by one, and I was quickly smiling again and I was fueled with absolute joy. It was a reminder that through my pain, I found inner peace, true love, joy and happiness. I carefully sealed the box anticipating all of the love that our future holds. I paused and I said another prayer to God—this time it was a prayer of thanksgiving.

Nighttime had fallen, and it was getting late. I walked towards the window to draw the curtains and relax, but as my hand reached out for the silk drape, my eyes gazed outside of the window and landed on a big, bright, glowing, full moon. I took a deep breath, and I admired the magnitude of its beauty. I slowly exhaled and softly smiled as I stared at the moon. I spoke in a tired voice, "Total dependence on God and God alone."

5/3/10

Lesson: Your mindset is critical to recovery and progress. Belief is your saving grace.

My dad went to Jackson, Mississippi to a special rehabilitation center. We were all excited about getting new ideas and opinions that could possibly help to further my father's progress. We wanted fresh eyes and new minds to hopefully offer new alternatives in his healing and recovery.

The facility is an in-patient care center, and my mother was very reluctant to leave my father by himself. She knows how dependent he is on her love, support and care. I encouraged and reminded her that it would be a great opportunity for her to have a little break. She needed to rest and have time to visit with her friends and just be; she literally has not left my father's side in two years. Reluctantly, she listened to me.

I believe the time that was given to her was difficult for her own personal reasons. Not only did she miss the presence of my dad as they have been together since they were fifteen years old, but she was awakened at how drastically her life had changed. She forgot what it was like to wake up without the responsibility of caring for someone else, taking walks without having to push a wheelchair, meeting friends on a whim and running errands without having to arrange for a caretaker, bathing only herself and simply living life in a way that we all take for granted—until you realize how very precious these "mundane" things really are. She misses the freedom of living life with such ease, but more than anything, she misses her life with my dad, as she once knew it. The reality of her new reality. Regardless of the challenges and changes, she would not have it any other way—she simply loves my dad!

In the meantime, my father was struggling with issues as well. His health was challenged by a new set of unfortunate circumstances, and he missed being home with my mother. To make matters worse, the doctors gave us news that we were not expecting to hear. They told my older brother, Patrick, that my dad's condition would not improve. You can only imagine how disheartening this was for my mother to hear. Upon receiving this news, we both sat on the edge of my bed, and my mom wept uncontrollably. She was heartbroken and emotionally worn out with their circumstance. The only thing I could do to comfort both of us was to remind ourselves of two very powerful words, God + Hope.

The next morning, as I was praying to God, my heart suddenly spoke, "Do not let your dad be discouraged. If he loses hope and does not believe he can overcome his circumstances, physically or emotionally, he never will. His belief is our saving grace."

5/10/10

Enjoy: Anticipation!

It's hard to believe my wedding is only four short weeks away. I'm counting down in great anticipation of what will be a glorious day! My love for Stanton only continues to grow stronger and I can literally feel my heart expand, contract and pull in every direction towards him. It feels like a beautiful, yet gentle growing pain. I smile and delight in knowing he feels the exact same way about me. We ache to be together and we yearn to be one—sharing life and living in love.

5/14/10

ONE JOURNEY IS ENDING, BUT A NEW ONE IS BEGINNING. RELAX AND ENJOY WHAT IS COMING YOUR WAY.

The movers are scheduled to come on Saturday. I needed a break from packing so I decided to head outside and go for a run. I walked out of the side door and made my way up the train tracks. As I did, I glanced over to the right and looked at Pontiff Park   a park that became so instrumental to my journey. My eyes filled up with tears as I thought about all of the hard work and beautiful moments I experienced with Jesus. Just as God would have it, I could no longer feel the pain (although I know it existed), all I could remember was the joy I found in each day. Jesus, always knowing my thoughts and feelings, quickly interjected, "One journey is ending, but a new one is beginning. Relax and enjoy what is coming to you." In my heart, I thanked Jesus and told Him how very much I appreciated all He does for me and my family and how very much I love and adore Him.

As I like to say, it saddens me when one journey of your life ends because even if it involves pain, it becomes a part of you—it is your life at that moment. What I have learned is that you must surrender yourself to the present, let go of the past, only bringing forward the wisdom you gained, and enjoy the present at last.

5/15/10

Prayer: Sweet Jesus, I pray that researchers and doctors are
             open to receive Your wisdom. I pray that a cure for
             cystic fibrosis is found.

My hospitalization reunited me with Joanna Nelson, Jo Beth's
mom. Today, there was a fundraiser for cystic fibrosis in Audubon
Park in New Orleans. Joanna told me about the fundraiser, and she
also informed me that Verna, Jo Beth's best friend, has a son who
was diagnosed with cystic fibrosis. Verna is pregnant again, and
her unborn child has been diagnosed with C.F. as well. You tell
me, what are the chances of your two children being diagnosed
with the very same illness that took the life of your best friend? My
belief is that God knew what Verna's future would hold, and He
wanted her to have the experience with Jo Beth in order to prepare
her for the challenges she would eventually face. Jo Beth would
serve not only as a friend, but also as a teacher. In return, Verna
would bring support and love to Jo Beth's life when she would
need it the most.

     My heart has been touched by these circumstances, and I
want to make finding a cure to cystic fibrosis one of my missions.

     How not ironic when I opened up my mailbox the other day I
found a letter in regards to supporting the Cystic Fibrosis
Foundation. In case you're wondering, "No, I did not give Joanna
my mailing address, nor had I spoken to Verna. It came to me as
some would say, "out of the blue." There are *no coincidences*.

     The letter is written by seven year old, "Rosie" who has been
diagnosed with C.F. She mentions that it is difficult to remember
and pronounce, "Cystic Fibrosis" so she calls it "64 Roses." After I
read her letter to my daughters they told me we should pray for
Rosie and 64 Roses every night. They added, "We are going to tell

all of our friends about this at school tomorrow and they can pray with us."

Today, me, Susan, Sophia, my parents, my sister-in-law Stephanie, and her two children—Kate and Stone met Joanna, her husband, Tom and Verna at Audubon Park to walk for a cure for 64 Roses! As we approached the park, Susan and Sophia asked, "Mommy is Rosie going to be here? We want to meet her!"

My prayer today is for all of the families who are suffering from cystic fibrosis. I pray, in the name of Jesus and through the intercession of Mary, to enlighten and infuse the minds of researchers and doctors who are working on a cure. I pray they are open to receive God's wisdom and knowledge. I pray that a cure is found in the near future.

Jo Beth, this one is for you!

5/30/10

Lesson: TIME will tell what God has planned for you. Be patient.

The girls and I are moving to Houston on Tuesday. Stanton and I leased a house in Houston, and it is appointed with everything that I prayed for—a convenient location, it rests upon a beautiful lot surrounded by trees (which is hard to find in town), it's open to the outdoors with walls of windows, it has a great floor plan (with room to grow!), it's in close proximity to work and the girls school, it has a swimming pool to cool down from the blazing Texas sun (which is already surrounded by a baby gate!) and it has his and her offices located right next to each other (as Stanton and I both office from home). What more could we possibly need? I hear, "Ask and you shall receive!"

The house has great potential for a renovation. Who knows, maybe we will have the means to buy it one day. For now, I am only focusing on living together as a loving family and, possibly a growing one. God willing, I accept the challenge! Stanton is so eager to be a father—he wants a honeymoon baby! I have given it more thought. My thinking is, *It would be so nice to enjoy some time just being us and keeping it simple.* What I have learned is that God's plans, and His timing is always better than mine. With that said, I am going to continue to live in the moment and allow God to work His way, God's Way. Time will tell what He has planned for us...

6/5/10

Lesson: God reveals Himself to everyone, pay attention!

Our wedding celebration has arrived, and it is an absolutely beautiful day! What an amazing feeling when the very moment you have been longing for finally arrives—it is no longer just a thought or a dream, it is reality!

The rehearsal dinner was last night. It was a very special moment for both me and Stanton to have an opportunity to stand up before our families, and talk about the God-given love we've been blessed with. It is fun to see how Stanton and I are teaching each other. Stanton, who often forgets to just go with what the day brings (without planning anything) came unprepared. He said he has never been unprepared for a speech but he simply wanted to speak what came naturally, from his heart. As for myself, I like to speak what comes to my heart, but Stanton has been teaching me how to plan. I came equipped with handwritten notes, and I was hungry to speak. Wanting to set the tone, I quickly stood up at the rehearsal dinner and this is what I said:

> "I am truly grateful to not only have the knowledge of true love, but to have the experience, and for this, I am grateful to God. The events that led up to our encounter are extremely significant because they reveal God's hand at work. You all know the depth of my spirituality and the importance that it brings to my life. In my opinion, it is not about showing up at church on Sunday, memorizing and reciting verses from the Bible, fearing church rules and regulations or putting on a 'Christian' image for a public persona. For me, life is *truly* about living God's

will, being intimate with Him, sharing my life with Him and trusting Him in all ways.

So, as I journeyed out into the world as a single woman, I knew I would need help. Although I was already full in spirit, love and peace—I wanted to share it with someone special, and I didn't want just anyone. I specifically asked Jesus and Mary to lead me to my soul mate, a life partner. I thought I knew what I wanted, but I had the wisdom to know that God knew what I needed. They say that luck happens when time meets preparation. Jesus knew that I was not prepared for the opportunity before me: the chance at experiencing true love with a life partner.

One year prior to meeting Stanton, my training and preparation began. God knew that I would need His help in tackling this 6'4", 220-pound cowboy that would soon be coming my way! Fortunately, I allowed Jesus to lead me and to teach me, and this is how it all began.

#1. I was instructed to lose control in order to gain God's control. Although this sounds easy and most people will SAY that they trust in God, I rarely believe that they are actually LIVING their words. I know, from experience, that it takes every morsel of will power to actually become powerless. I believe it goes against our human instincts, but I was determined to live the life that God designed for me. I was sternly told, 'Total dependence on God and God alone.'

#2. I was taught to detach myself from other people's opinions. I was told that this would also specifically pertain to someone that I would fall in love with—I was to listen only to God. God knew how I always sought approval from others. He wanted me to seek Him above all others. God is the only being I ever need approval from.

#3. I was instructed not to focus on the 'faults' of others because there are no 'faults.' There are only differences. Who are we to judge? Who are we to think that our way of living is the way to life? It is God that made us different—and for good reasons. I was told to embrace and learn from differences, focus on the positive and focus on love.

#4. And then, of course, there is 'Let It Be!' The words, "Whispering words of wisdom, let it be, let it be..." had been revealed to me many times during prayer and meditation, and I knew that Jesus was trying to tell me something. I knew the song, and the words held great significance. The significance was finally revealed to me when Stanton and I reunited at the River Oaks Country Club Tennis Tournament for the first time in over twenty years. As we sat down at a table to talk, the band who had been on a break came back at the *very same time* and immediately they started playing, "Let It Be" by the Beatles. Stanton, sitting next to me, looked me in the eyes, and he began to sing the words to me. He stopped, mid-song and asked, 'Do you know this song?' At that very moment I knew that this meeting was not by chance, but by purpose. This was my clue from God to take action on His direction. It was His sign to me that the opportunity I had been asking Him for was sitting right before me—the opportunity to find true love in a life partner. I asked God for His help. Now, it was my turn to trust Him enough to take His lead.

I once read, 'The perfect person is never perfect. Perfection lies in PERCEPTION.'

It's interesting that most of the characteristics that can be viewed by others as 'faults' of Stanton, or 'differences' as God refers to them are the very traits that I fell in love with and the very traits that I appreciate the most.

Living life—Stanton truly lives life to the absolute fullest capacity! It is impossible to not have fun with him! There is not one day that passes without him making me laugh. Some may view this trait as a lack of seriousness or lack of responsibility, but for me, the worker-bee, he is my reminder to slow down and enjoy life by letting loose and living large because we only have one chance.

Honesty. Stanton speaks the truth. He literally verbalizes his every innermost thought. Some may view this trait as rude and offensive…and, although he could soften his choice of words on occasion, I embrace this characteristic! As the old saying goes, 'The truth hurts.' And…it usually does, but what I have learned from experience is that I would rather be hurt by the truth than be hurt by a lie. It takes more courage to speak honestly than it does to hide behind deceit. Another benefit…do you know how nice it is to constantly hear someone tell you their innermost thoughts, especially when they are filled with love and appreciation! It is so nice to know every time he simply thinks about me, how much he loves and adores me, how special and beautiful he thinks I am. The list goes on and on, and it is never-ending. Stanton sings love to me!

Courage. Stanton simply has no fear. He is never one to shy away from the big elephant in the room. He confronts the situation head on, standing up to his beliefs and verbalizing his honest opinions. Some may view this trait as confrontational or bullying, but I see it is as taking a stand. Most importantly, it is Stanton's innermost courage that I admire the most. The courage to admit when he is wrong, the courage to apologize, the courage in accepting consequences and the courage to make the necessary changes within himself because he wants to be a better man.

Tender. Yes, I just used that sweet adjective to describe Stanton, and I want to say it again, tender! Believe it or not, when you have the patience to listen beyond his often loud and harsh words, you will find the most loving, sweet, gentle and loyal soul. His actions speak even louder than his words and they have shown me nothing but the greatest love, tenderness, peace, protection and care. I have also finally found someone who is as affectionate as I am…hugs and kisses, hugs and kisses, they never end!

Positive. No matter how difficult or disappointed Stanton's circumstances are he confronts them with all of his energy. He wants legitimate answers and explanations. Eventually, he makes peace with the outcome, even when the outcome is not what he hoped for. Some may see this as a lack of care or concern, but I see it as his understanding that there will be disappointments in life, but dwelling on them or trying to control them will not change the outcome. He simply surrenders to the situation, remembering that he has a life to live, happily and to the fullest.

Loyalty. Stanton loves family and friends. No matter what the differences are, he accepts and loves each for who they are. He understands that every person has a different relationship, but he never allows someone else's issues to become his own. He bases his relationships on his experience only. Stanton also told me early in our relationship that he is the man that would always love me and that he would never leave my side. He had the opportunity to put his words into action when I had my internal bleed…and he never left my side. He sat next to me holding my hand, encouraging me to fight, praying with me and telling me how much he loves me, staring into my swollen and beaten eyes whispering how beautiful I am, but that it is my heart that he is truly after. Every night, he slept in the chair next to my hospital bed, only leaving the room to shower and eat. He begged every doctor to 'save me' as he would explain that it took him forty years to find me and that he couldn't lose me now.

And, finally, love. It is the first word that comes to my heart when I think about Stanton. His heart is a treasure, and it was waiting to be discovered. I thank God for showing me where it is."

As I sat down in my chair to pray and meditate on May 10, 2010, I thought about what I wanted to say on this very night. I looked at Jesus's picture standing before me, and I asked Him for His help in guiding my words. I was doing a Beth Moore Bible study on the disciple, John, and the book, *John, 90 Days with the Beloved Disciple*, was sitting at the table to the left of me. I felt His Spirit encourage me to open it up. I randomly opened it to page 157. It is an entry I wrote on June 4, 2009, *exactly one year prior to the eve of my wedding with Stanton*! The question posed was this: "We are built for adventure. And, often, the only thing that keeps us from embarking on one is that it comes disguised as an average day. What kind of adventure with Christ might be waiting for you before sundown tomorrow if you were looking for it? Just imagine…"

I closed my eyes and this is what I saw, exactly one year ago to this very day. I wrote, "Before sundown tomorrow…awaits an adventure that I have always dreamed of. An adventure of love, excitement, happiness, joy, peace and comfort. A place of knowing truth in your heart, both giving and receiving, supporting, nurturing and including God and sharing HIS love, in one another. Asking God to be present in all ways. Allowing God to guide for an eternity."

So, this is when I say, God reveals Himself to everyone, *if we pay attention*. He guided my thoughts into my future, and my dream is coming true.

June 6, 2010

Celebrate: "Here is to dreams and visions coming true."

Saturday, June 5, 2010 was another gorgeous day! We both felt excitement and disbelief that the "time" had finally arrived. We wanted to cherish every moment of this precious day, so Stanton suggested we take our golf cart on a cruise around the beautiful property. We stopped by the heart-shaped pond where he proposed to me so we could make a wedding day wish. I thought it was a great idea. Before walking out of the casita, I opened my wallet, blindly reached in the coin pocket and I pulled out a new, sparkling copper penny dated 2010. I thought to myself, "Perfect!" and I clenched it in the palm of my right hand, and Stanton and I happily kissed.

After driving around for some time and exploring the land, we finally came upon the pond. Stanton slowed down to park as he said, "This is where it all began." We wanted to capture the moment, so Stanton pulled out his camera and we instinctively put our heads closely together. We stood still, cheek to cheek, smiling widely as Stanton stretched his long arm out in front of us and snapped a few pictures.

The grass still held the morning dew and my feet were wet by the time we reached the water's edge. We gazed out across the pond, and we slowly turned to face each other—we looked into each other's eyes and once again, we asked God to please bless our marriage with peace, love, health, happiness, and time. Together, we tossed the bright, copper penny high up into the air, and it flew far across the water. We kissed, and we held each other tightly as we softly professed our love to one another.

We drove back to the main building. We were greeted with a beautifully prepared breakfast that was waiting for us outside under the veranda. We spoke few words as we ate our food and enjoyed just being. My eyes gazed across the infinity pool and what appears to be an endless amount of peaceful land, rolling hills and beautiful horses roaming freely and happily, I thought to myself, "God, please tell me this is a picture of my future."

Within a few short hours, our quiet little haven that had only consisted of Stanton .and I resting on the lawn chairs was soon filled with family, friends and children's laughter. We swam, ate, drank, had golf cart races with the kids, explored the property and simply enjoyed our amazing surroundings. All day, Stanton and I were completely relaxed because we were just ready, ready because it is so right and so…meant to be.

At 2:00 p.m. we all headed back to our casitas to get dressed for the ceremony and celebration. Susan, Sophia and I were pleasantly surprised as we walked in our room, only to find some of my most precious friends waiting to surprise us. They were equipped with hugs, kisses, laughter and champagne. They all laughed, "Katie, only you would still be in your bathing suit, not dressed and completely calm two hours before your wedding. Not to mention, you are doing your own hair and makeup!" I laughed and I said, "Yes, that is *so me*!" We made a toast and we all sipped champagne and I finally got dressed. They assisted me by helping Susan and Sophia with their hair and dresses, all the while keeping the mood fun and light. I almost cried when I saw the girls in their white ballerina style dresses accented with a large, yellow sash. They truly looked like little angels, and I felt so grateful to have such loving daughters to share this very special moment with.

As the time drew near, I slipped into the dress that I designed, and I finished the look off by borrowing long Chanel pearls that my brother, Christopher, had given to my sister-in-law, Stephanie, a shorter strand of pearls that my father had given me for my sixteenth birthday and my gold medal of Our Lady of Mt. Carmel that Stanton gave me for my birthday last year. The medal is a representation of love and dedication to Jesus, and the desire to live God's will—my dress was now complete.

At 4:00 p.m., I was ready. I sat calmly in the window of my casita, and we began to watch the caravan of cars winding down the long, gravel road to gather for the cocktail reception. I soon felt butterflies fluttering around in my belly, and I was anxious to see Stanton standing at the end of the rose garden, waiting for me, so we could spend our lives together for an eternity.

Finally, at 5:15 p.m., the phone in my casita rang. Susan ran over to answer it, "Hello. Okay, I will get her for you. Mommy, it's Jennifer!" I took the phone from Susan's hand, "Hello!" and I quickly heard, "Katie, everyone is ready for you. Start making your way over to the garden." And I responded anxiously, "Okay. Great!" I turned to Susan, Sophia and a dear friend of mine who was still waiting with us, Lisa and her daughter, Hannah, who is like a daughter to me, and Susan's best friend. I looked at everyone, "They're ready! Let's go!" We all gathered around, held hands and we said a sweet prayer together.

As I approached the rose garden that was now in full bloom, I could see the white wooden chairs occupied by our guests, and they rested peacefully upon the manicured green grass. Stanton looked so handsome as he smiled proudly standing in front of the trellis with his shoulders back and his head held up high—he was dressed in a classic khaki summer suit, a crisp white dress shirt, a bright orange tie and a coordinating pocket square. Standing by his side was his best man and father, Gene Scott and the minister, Alan. As I stood at the end of the garden, I could not stop smiling. I held onto a blue Miraculous Medal of Mary that was tied to my simple bouquet of yellow roses. I placed my thumb upon the medal, and I rubbed it gently as I thanked Mary for being with me in spirit. My three handsome brothers approached me with hugs and kisses, and they sweetly escorted me down the aisle to greet my father who was waiting for me in his wheelchair that was parked in the front row. I leaned over towards him, and as he kissed me, he said, "I love you, Katie." He stretched out his hand to give me away to Stanton, who was waiting for me with tears in his eyes. Full of emotions, we faced each other, both of us were beaming with joy. We held hands tightly, and Stanton leaned into me and whispered, "Here is to dreams and visions coming true." I nodded my head in agreement, thinking to myself, "Yes, God, we did it!" I smiled back at him in complete and perfect fulfillment— my inner being was bursting at the seams and I felt as if I was literally overflowing with love, happiness and spiritual graces.

Alan spoke about Jesus and the wedding at Cana, he read from Ecclesiastes, "There is an appointed time for everything, and a time for every affair under the heavens..." and he touched on a few of the personal stories that Stanton and I had shared with him. He mentioned how his curiosity gave way when I told him about my experience, and the significant timing of the appearance of the red cardinal. He said that after our meeting, he went home and asked his wife if she knew what the meaning was, and it eventually led them to research and discover that the red cardinal is a representation of Christmas—the color, red, is a representation of the blood of Christ. He also spoke about Stanton showing me his loyalty, in sickness and in health, and how God taught him patience, as he waited for me for forty years. As the ceremony proceeded, we all laughed as Stanton's dad fumbled through all of his pockets trying to locate the ring. Stanton, now getting *impatient*, jokingly exclaimed, "Come on, Geno, I've only been waiting forty-one years for this woman!" Finally, he found the ring, and he handed it to me, but I accidentally dropped it in the grass and had to retrieve it! After the laughter died down, we shifted gears. We exchanged our vows with heartfelt meaning, and the ceremony ended with Alan, happily declaring, "...you may kiss the bride!" Stanton, full of energy and excitement, surprisingly dipped me close to the ground, and we happily kissed. We walked down the aisle, as husband and wife, as the string quartet played to the tune of "Viva la Vida" by Coldplay.

The reception was understandably hot, as we gathered under the blazing June Texas sun, but regardless, it was absolutely perfect! The food was above and beyond the word exceptional— the chef prepared tuna sashimi encrusted in sesame and black pepper, rack of lamb served with Israeli couscous and vegetables, filet, garlic mashed potatoes and beefsteak tomatoes and buffalo mozzarella cheese. As you can probably guess, Stanton and I danced to "Let it be" for our first dance as a married couple. We also put in a special request for the New Orleans' Saints theme song, "Crunk." Together, with family and friends, we all danced through thick smoke and laser lights, and I felt as if I was dancing in a sea of puffy clouds in heaven!

The night came to an end, and Stanton took over the D.J.'s microphone and announced, "This is dedicated to my wife, Katie, because she lights up my life!" Night had fallen, and I stood closely to Stanton in great anticipation of what was before us…explosive fireworks soon began to light up the dark sky. It was an unexpected, beautiful and powerful moment, and it felt as if it lasted forever. I smiled and laughed as I shouted into the sky while placing my hands on my belly, "Lord, bless this womb!" I hugged Stanton and told him how much I appreciate his enthusiasm—we kissed (imagine that) and Stanton took me by the hand and led the way…

We thanked our family and friends as we said goodbye—a horse and carriage awaited us, and we happily climbed in. We looked at each other, let out a sigh of relief and exclaimed, "We did it! It's all over. Now, we can just be!" As we approached our casita, Stanton looked at me, "I love you, Mrs. Scott!" I replied, "I love you, Mr. Scott!" We smiled and laughed. Stanton stepped out of the carriage, lifted me up and happily carried me over the threshold.

Cheers to happy endings…and to new beginnings!

6/8/10

Dear God,

I am writing You a thank You note as Stanton and I lay peacefully on the beach at Cap Juluca in Anguilla. We are on our honeymoon! The beauty that I feel inside and the beauty that surrounds me is exactly how I imagine heaven to be…

I look in front of me and all I can see is water that is so blue and crystal clear, and gentle mountains serve as the backdrop. It is sunny, quite, peaceful, and the people are friendly. There is a sailboat smoothly sailing across the water and it radiates happy and fun colors that consist of blue, yellow and red. The sand is white, soft and free of debris. I glance to my left and I see a copy of our book that I have brought along for editing, design magazines, bottled water, sun-screen and, of course, Stanton, who is resting peacefully under our umbrella.

I will never be able to express to You, in written words, the appreciation, love and respect that I have for You. I can only promise to show You my gratitude by living my life accordingly, and striving to sow every seed that You planted in me. How wasteful it would be to not complete your design. I can't imagine anyone wanting to bury their diamond and not enjoy the beauty and radiance that it is intended to bring.

Thank You for showing me how to give and receive healthy love and for bringing my soul sheer joy and happiness; for teaching me more than I ever imagined I could learn and definitely more than I ever thought I would experience with You while living on earth. I simply would not be sitting here, in this peaceful state of heart and mind, if my life had not been placed in Your loving and protecting Hands. I am so grateful that Jesus gave me, through His Spirit, the wisdom to CHOOSE YOU, to CHOOSE LIFE and to CHOOSE LOVE.

I hope that our story will lead lost souls to You. I pray that they give You the opportunity to show them what they are looking for. I pray that they give You the time, patience, endurance and discipline that is required. I pray that they do not see You as a "quick fix" to their challenges but rather, a way to life. I pray that we always remember, "We learn to live differently by DOING THINGS DIFFERENTLY, not by THINKING about living differently."

God, I look forward to our journey, together, one day at a time. I am not just a dreamer...I am a believer.

Yours truly,

LET IT BE! Mr and Mrs Stanton Scott! Wedding day at Dos Brisas, June 05, 2010!

My amazingly strong and loving parents, Susan and David Ridgeway,
celebrating with me and Stanton.

My angel daughters and flower girls, Susan and Sophia.

My brothers, Patrick, Christopher "Critter" and Michael Ridgeway. I cherish them!